Living Scripture

By Mary Chadwick Wolff

PRESS

If you have any questions or comments, feel free to email them to:

LivingScriptureBook@gmail.com

www.xulonpress.com

To Anne,

Who loves to read. May
you be blessed by reading
this one.

Love,

Mary

I dedicate this work to my children.

Hear, O Israel: The LORD our God, the LORD is one. Love the LORD your God with all your heart and with all your soul and with all your strength. These commandments that I give you today are to be upon your hearts. Impress them on your children. Talk about them when you sit at home and when you walk along the road, when you lie down and when you get up. Tie them as symbols on your hands and bind them on your foreheads. Write them on the doorframes of your houses and on your gates.

Deuteronomy 6:4-9

Acknowledgements

I am so blessed by my family. They have made my life so enjoyable and shaped me into a much better person. I appreciate their willingness to allow me to expose such personal details about their lives for this book. They were also very helpful throughout the writing process with Anna and Peter encouraging me to persevere through the difficult times. I am also grateful for John revising my initial attempts and especially for Paul who did extensive editing on several occasions to make my book much more readable.

I would like to thank all of the many people who answered my plea to pray over the writing of this book. Mary, Jeanne, Ruth, and those at the Christian Missionary and Alliance church, where I attended for years, come most readily to mind. I am also so thankful that God seemingly put Bob in my life to peruse this book. He especially encouraged me and cheered me onward towards its completion.

I am thankful to all those who have walked beside me during all of my trials, which helped me to maintain my sanity during such difficult times. I am most grateful for my next door neighbors, Jo and Patti. They truly were the Lord's hands and feet to me as they helped me carry my burdens through the tough times.

I am also appreciative of other fellow Christians who have shared their spiritual insights with me. God loves to see people relate to each other and, by helping each other, we gain a better understanding of the many of mysteries of the Bible.

Most of all, I praise the Lord. I glorify Him that He saw fit that I could serve Him by undertaking this project, and for the grace to complete it. I am amazed that the Almighty Creator of this world wants to have intimate relationships with us and offers us each a covenant of eternal salvation. How great is the God we have!

Contents

Preface

Write a book...

    I felt the Lord calling me to write but I hated writing. I ignored it and let a year pass...

Write a book...

    Ugh, I really did not feel gifted as a writer. I ignored it again and let another year pass...

Write a book!

    Every time I would pray about what God wanted me to do for Him, the message was always the same—*Write a book!* I knew that the Lord was calling me to convey how He had worked in my life. Yet to me, the thought of writing these experiences in a book seemed beyond my abilities, and so I choose to ignore His promptings. However, I continued to feel the pressure to write for a few years until this feeling eventually became burdensome. Fearing that I was becoming disobedient, I eventually began this project.

Producing a book solely about my life stories seemed so self-centered, even if my intention was to reveal God's glory. Therefore, I initially wanted to add separate spiritual lessons to accompany each section followed by supporting Scripture. However, doing so made the work too lengthy. In the end, I decided just to embed some of the spiritual lessons within my narratives.

The project took me almost ten years to complete. Even though I attempted to tithe my time, there were many periods when I failed to work on it at all. Finally, I found myself with a deadline from the publisher and even resigned from my job to complete it, trusting that I was indeed following God's command.

Over the years, I asked many people to pray over this project. It is my greatest hope that by reading this book you will desire to draw close to the Lord, especially through reading His Word and trying to obey what he wants you to do in your life. Then, as you learn to rely on God's power, He will enlighten and guide you, transforming how you live your own life into *living Scripture*.

Salvation

" If you would like to commit your life to the Lord, come down to the front of the church," the speaker encouraged. I wanted to go forward but my feet seemed glued to the floor. I watched as others slowly navigated their way to the waiting guides who whisked them off to a more private place to converse while I remained in my seat. I felt turmoil within my soul between going up to make a commitment and staying in my seat. My uncertainty persisted until the program ended about five minutes later. Relieved that I could escape this uncomfortable feeling, I quickly made my way out of the church and onto the bus that had brought me.

I was living in State College, Pennsylvania at this time, having recently graduated from Pennsylvania State University. Some guy had befriended me and invited me to attend this event with him. It was located in Bellefonte, a small community about half an hour away from the college.

Once seated on the bus beside this boy, the pressure resurfaced as he pressed, "Are you sure that you don't want to turn your life over to Jesus?" It sounded like a reasonable thing to do, but some type of barrier existed that I just could not cross over in my mind.

Years passed before another chance presented itself for me to surrender my life to God. I was taking summer classes at Indiana State University of Pennsylvania trying to obtain the necessary credits beyond my bachelor's degree for permanent certification as a teacher in Pennsylvania. I was staying in the dorms at the university and someone walked down the hallway where I was staying inviting people to come. They called into any open door, "Would you want to come to a fellowship gathering of students?"

I believed only lonely and vulnerable students would ever accept such an offer. I declined, taking pride in myself for not getting tricked into what I believed was some cult-like group.

My reluctance was not because I didn't believe in God. Instead, as I reflect back now, I conclude it was because I was never exposed to the love that God had for me. I never read the Bible and rarely tried to have a connection with God through prayer. Maybe more importantly, I never witnessed His concern for me as He acted through others guided by the Holy Spirit.

My ideas of religion were mostly formulated from growing up in the Catholic Church. Although my mother was Methodist, when she had married my Catholic father, the Catholic Church required her to sign a paper stating that any children produced by their union would be brought up in the Catholic faith. She attended her own church while my father and I faithfully marched off to a Catholic church.

The Catholic church that I attended was filled with well-intentioned people. However, in my mind, that church completely missed the motives of God. It promoted a, "Do this," "Avoid doing that," kind of ideology, without consulting God to His specific desires. The only type of personal prayer that was practiced was one where we asked to receive something from God according to our own desires. They never prayed to glorify Him or seek His will. I rarely thought to praise Him or even thank Him for the blessings in my life. I understood that there were rules of how to live peaceably with others and, if I generally followed those guidelines, I would be considered a "good person." This would earn me the right to go to heaven when I passed away. These beliefs made me picture God as a supreme being who was only interested in enforcing rules on me. Since I believed I had things in my life that I felt I would have to stop doing in order to please Him, I was hesitant to submit to Him.

This guilt-producing approach produced little passion for God from me or my siblings. My brother and sister refused to attend Mass by the time they reached high school. In the same way, when I satisfied all my youthful religious requirements set forth by the Catholic Church, my attendance at Mass slowly dwindled as well. Spending energy on achieving good grades, having fun with friends, and catching up on some much-needed sleep were more attractive options to me.

Instead of attending church during my high school years, Sunday night dinners with my family became an outlet for religious thought and discussion. My brother and sister, who were now both out of school and living on their own, returned home each weekend for a home-cooked meal and time with the family. Around the table, we would discuss religious ideas. My older brother Richard had become influenced by the Eastern religions that were then popular in some circles of the youth culture. He promoted such ideas as "God is in everything," and, "You control your own destiny." These statements spurred many debates in my family and we referred to encyclopedias and other books frequently to support our arguments. Although influenced somewhat by these heated discussions, I mostly retained many of my earlier beliefs from the Catholic Church.

The Lord, however, continued to stand at the door of my heart and knock. Five months after I married my high school sweetheart, David, we moved into Maple Ridge Townhouses. It was there that I first experienced the magnetic Christ-like love and caring from believers in my life.

In this neighborhood, women often gathered in the cul-de-sac in front of our townhouse and chatted together as their children played. One day, after returning home from my job as a home economics teacher, I chose to walk over to join them. While we were talking, one of the women casually mentioned, "Money has been tight, but the Lord has been providing for us." That statement really took me aback. I hardly knew this woman, yet she had the audacity to mention God, something I believed should only be discussed only within the four walls of a church building. It was fine to believe in a supreme being, but talking about Him in casual conversation was just odd, I thought.

As I became better acquainted with my neighbors, I learned that this woman who had spoken so freely about

God let Christ permeate everything in her life. Her name was also Mary. Her house was decorated with all sorts of religious items and Christian music often streamed from her kitchen window. She prayed over everything, even asking me to join in with her once when her son fell down and got hurt. She and her husband held Bible studies in their home, one of which she invited David and me to attend. However, I was still unsure of it all, and we graciously declined.

Mary and the other women in this cul-de-sac did many other thoughtful acts for me. After arriving home from a particularly long day of teaching during the Christmas season, I found a tin of spritz cookies sitting on my doorstep that another neighbor, Debbie, had made. Ann, Karen, and Charlene frequently invited me over for lunch and were considerate in other ways as well. Mary and Denise even threw baby showers for me when I became pregnant with my first two children.

I often wondered why these women were so kind to me. I had not done anything to deserve such pleasantries. I was used to just looking out for myself and not being concerned with anyone else's needs. Yet, these women were always seeking to include me in their activities and offering to help me in any way they could.

Their behavior influenced me, and it wasn't long until I began to mimic them. I attempted to do caring acts for them as well. I started listening to Christian radio and vowed to read a chapter from the Bible each morning. I struggled to fully understand the Bible, but I continued, believing it would be good to read the Scripture at least once all the way through.

Even with my neighbors' influences, I didn't begin attending church until after my husband and I had our first child in April 1983. My husband and I had a girl who we named Anna. Having Anna made me nostalgic about my own childhood, so I attempted to re-create some of my own childhood memories for her. I quit my job and conjured up images of Anna going to church and attending CCD classes. I sought out the nearest Catholic church, which turned out to be St. Steven's. It was just down the road and was a rapidly growing congregation with many young families.

Although David had also grown up going to church, he chose not to attend with us at first. However, he seemed uncomfortable about our participation in this religious activity without him. After our first couple of visits, David started to question me about our church-going. "Who do you see there? What was the sermon about?" Maybe he was experiencing a bit of guilt for not going himself. Whatever the motivation, it was not long before he joined us.

God is creative and calls each person in a unique manner. It can occur after hearing someone preach about obtaining eternal life and then that person submits their life to Him. Others come to a point where they find themselves in an overwhelming situation and are desperate for relief. Having no other place to turn, they cry out to God for help and then, after He answers, they feel compelled to follow Him. Some fortunate ones may have a divine intervention where they immediately feel the hand of God, such as the time when God calls Saul in the Bible. Still others, like me, are magnetically attracted to God by witnessing Christ-like behavior from others, which motivates them to seek Him.

Whatever way God calls a person they, at some point, come to the realization that their sins separate them from God. They also realize that they are incapable of avoiding sinning, and He is perfect and cannot be in the presence of sin. Being apart from God, they would be doomed to spend eternity apart from Him after they die. Yet, God provided a way for our sins to be washed away through the shedding of blood. Under the Old Covenant, a person confessed their transgressions and then the priest would slaughter an animal to remove the due penalty of sin. Then, in the fullness of time, God sent His Son, Jesus, to die on a cross as the perfect final sacrifice, instead of continually being required to slay an animal. Anyone acknowledging this act would have their sins covered by Jesus' blood, thus permanently restoring their connection with God.

This realization for me completely changed my life. During my Christian walk, I gradually shifted from focusing on earthly concerns to more eternal issues. I wanted to focus on what God desired me to accomplish in this life. I found peace and assurance that had previously escaped me. Relationships with other Christians gained depth and a closeness that I had not experienced before in a friendship. I was able to experience joy, even during the most challenging events in my life since I knew that this life was not the final chapter. Death was not something to fear but would allow me to spend the rest of eternity with my Creator who only had love for me.

Scripture

John 3:16: For God so loved the world that he gave his one and only Son, that whoever believes in him shall not perish but have eternal life.

John 14:6: Jesus answered, "I am the way and the truth and the life. No one comes to the Father except through me."

Hebrews 9:11-28:

When Christ came as high priest of the good things that are already here, he went through the greater and more perfect tabernacle that is not man-made, that is to say, not a part of this creation. He did not enter by means of the blood of goats and calves; but he entered the Most Holy Place once for all by his own blood, having obtained eternal redemption. The blood of goats and bulls and the ashes of a heifer sprinkled on those who are ceremonially unclean sanctify them so that they are outwardly clean. How much more, then, will the blood of Christ, who through the eternal Spirit offered himself unblemished to God, cleanse our consciences from acts that lead to death, so that we may serve the living God!

For this reason Christ is the mediator of a new covenant, that those who are called may receive the promised eternal inheritance—now that he has died as a ransom to set them free from the sins committed under the first covenant.

In the case of a will, it is necessary to prove the death of the one who made it, because a will is in force only when somebody has died; it never takes effect while the one who made it is living. This is why even the first covenant was not put into effect without blood. When Moses had proclaimed every commandment of the law to all the people, he took the blood of calves, together with water, scarlet wool and branches of hyssop, and sprinkled the scroll and all the people. He said, "This is the blood of the covenant, which God has commanded you to keep." In the same way, he sprinkled with the blood both the tabernacle and everything used in its ceremonies. In fact, the law requires that nearly everything be cleansed with blood and without the shedding of blood there is no forgiveness.

It was necessary, then, for the copies of the heavenly things to be purified with these sacrifices, but the heavenly things themselves with better sacrifices than these. For Christ did not enter a man-made sanctuary that was only a copy of the true one; he entered heaven itself, now to appear for us in God's presence. Nor did he enter heaven to offer himself again and again, the way the high priest enters the Most Holy Place every year with blood that is not his own. Then Christ would have had to suffer many times since the creation of the world. But now he has appeared once for all at the end of the ages to do away with sin by the sacrifice of himself. Just as man is destined to die once, and after that to face judgment, so Christ was sacrificed once to take away the sins of many people; and he will appear a second time, not to bear sin, but to bring salvation to those who are waiting for him.

1 John 4:7: Dear friends, let us love one another, for love comes from God. Everyone who loves has been born of God and knows God.

1 John 4:12: No one has ever seen God; but if we love one another, God lives in us and his love is made complete in us.

1 Peter 2:12: Live such good lives among the pagans that, though they accuse you of doing wrong, they may see your good deeds and glorify God on the day he visits us.

—2—

Spiritual Baptism

E ven though I was regularly attending St. Steven's Catholic Church, reading my Bible daily, praying more frequently, I was still not at the point where I was confident that I would eventually spend eternity with God. Arriving at that point was a gradual process that came as I deepened my relationship with God. One particular event really increased my closeness with Him and increased my confidence that I was truly saved. That event was my spiritual baptism.

I had not sought getting baptized in the Spirit, but it happened because I desired to get more involved in my church. I chose to sign up for some random class they were offering, but it was canceled because of lack of interest. I vowed to enroll in whatever course would be offered next, which turned out to be a "Life in the Spirit" seminar. I hardly gave much thought to its content—I just knew that it met once a week for six weeks and that Father Ken, the head priest of the parish, was sponsoring it.

When I arrived for the first session, I found out that participants from former sessions led the proceedings. The meeting opened with us singing a variety of spiritual songs lead by a man playing a guitar. Then, a speaker got up and spoke about how God had acted amazingly in his life. When he concluded his story, we were broken up into groups and given a spiritual question to discuss. After sharing our opinions, we were dismissed to have refreshments and fellowship.

The first three sessions followed this same format, but when we arrived for the fourth week, the leaders informed us that we would not be having a regular class. Instead, we would be making the sacrament of reconciliation in preparation for being "baptized in the Spirit" the following week. I had no idea what being "baptized in the Spirit" meant and the leaders offered few insights. The booklet we were instructed to read daily for the class made little reference to what this rite was. Instead it mostly contained Scripture that spoke of God's love for us and His desire to connect with us.

After the leaders shared this information with us, they told us to proceed to a room in the church where the confessionals were located. Once there, I grabbed one of the booklets designed to prepare people for this sacrament of reconciliation. Within its pages were listed many possible sins a person could commit. I skimmed over them, hoping to jog my memory of my past transgressions. After composing a list in my mind, I joined one of the confessional lines and tried to avoid the priest who had a tendency to be unsympathetic toward misbehavior. After confessing and being absolved of my sins, I headed home.

Since I now had two children, Anna and Peter, and was very busy, I gave very little thought to my upcoming "baptism." When the night of the Mass arrived, and I choose to dress as I normally would for a Sunday service. I donned a skirt and sweater and went downstairs to bid goodbye to my husband and his sister, who was visiting our family from out of town. They were going to stay home to visit and babysit the children.

As I drove to the church, I began to reflect on what being baptized in the Spirit could possibly mean. I had only heard of infants being baptized with water. Being baptized in the Spirit sounded so mystical and mysterious. However, I trusted that it must be legitimate because it was offered by a Catholic church.

After arriving at the church, I found a seat in the midsection of the church and waited for the proceedings to start. The Mass began as any other until it came time for the priest to deliver his sermon. Then, instead of the priest addressing the congregation, the coordinators of the seminar made their way to the front of the church and broke into groups of three or four. I intently watched, waiting for something to start. Someone announced, "Will those who wish to be baptized in the Spirit join a group one at a time?"

I was thankful I had chosen a seat that was further back so that I could see what was going to happen before it was my turn. I observed some of my fellow class members arising from their seats and heading toward these groups. Trying to take in all the details, I saw them each enter the formations and the group members encircle them. Then group members placed their hands on my classmates' shoulders and began to pray over them.

I anxiously watched and wondered what would happen next. After a short time, some of the people being prayed over began to gently fall backward, and the people who had been praying over them caught them and gently lowered them to the floor. *Oh, dear! What have I gotten myself into? I wished that I hadn't worn a skirt!*

When it was time for me to go forward, I was nervous about what was going to occur. However, I desired to receive whatever spiritual gift was being given, so I timidly proceeded down the center aisle and sought out an open group. As I approached one, the members all surrounded me. They placed their hands upon me and began to pray aloud. I put my head down and soaked in their prayers. I waited, but nothing out of the ordinary seemed to be happening. They continued to pray, but I began to fear that I was not worthy of such a blessing.

"Relax a bit," I heard one of the leaders say. I tried to, but I still did not feel anything special occurring. Then, after a little more time, it happened. I slowly began to sense a subtle impulse to incline backward. I knew I could fight it if I wished, but I relaxed and allowed it to occur. Those who had prayed over me guided me to a reclining position on the floor and then moved on to pray for someone else.

As I lay on the floor of the church, my eyes were closed, and I felt totally at peace. A warm, tingling sensation permeated my body. I was keenly aware of the music that was playing, as it seemed to have more depth than usual. I was captivated by this tranquil state and I felt so close to the Lord.

About ten minutes later, the intensity of this experienced lessened, and I opened my eyes and sheepishly retreated to my seat.

This experience totally transformed me and joy filled my heart as I drove home. I definitely knew something spiritual had occurred within me. When I arrived home, I was eager to tell David and his sister what had happened. They listened as I excitedly relayed my experience. However, my spiritual encounter was not received with as much delight by my husband, David, who was more skeptical.

"Sounds like some kind of cult to me. What is Father Ken doing in that church anyway?" David grumbled. It did seem rather strange, but I knew in my heart that this baptism was indeed from God and had drawn me closer to God. It gave me a passion to learn more about God and a new vigor to develop a relationship with Him.

Since I never had heard of being baptized with the Spirit before attending this seminar, I was curious if it was ever referred to in the Bible and so I viewed all passages that included the word "baptism." The first mention of baptism was John the Baptist carrying out the rite I was familiar with—a water baptism. Later in Acts 19:4, this baptism is described as one of repentance where one publicly admits that they are a sinner and are in need of a Savior. Luke 7:30 hints that unless one undergoes this act, God's purpose may not truly be fulfilled in a person's life. This verse states, "But the Pharisees and the experts in the law rejected God's purpose for themselves, because they had not been baptized by John."

Then, continuing to investigate, I saw this second type of baptism mentioned. The apostles appear to have experienced a spiritual baptism on the day of Pentecost as Acts 2:1-4 recognizes, "When the day of Pentecost came, they were all together in one place. Suddenly a sound like the blowing of a violent wind came from heaven and filled the whole house where they were sitting. They saw what seemed to be tongues of fire that separated and came to rest on each of them. All of them were filled with the Holy Spirit and began to speak in other tongues as the Spirit enabled them." This event apparently initiated mankind's ability to be filled with the Spirit. It was dramatic with a display of "tongues of fire," and everyone spoke in "other tongues" as they were enabled. Additionally, even though this group came from many different countries with various languages, the curious crowd that came together to witness this event heard them speaking in their own language.

After that day, other instances of spiritual baptisms are cited in Scripture. Acts 8:14-16 says, "When the apostles in Jerusalem heard that Samaria had accepted the word of God, they sent Peter and John to them. When they arrived, they prayed for them that they might receive the Holy Spirit, because the Holy Spirit had not yet come on any of them; they had simply been baptized in the name of the Lord Jesus." This passage illustrates that these new believers had undergone one type of baptism, and hints at this second type of baptism of the Spirit.

Additionally, Acts 18:24-26 also refers to this possible next step in the Christian walk. This passage describes a man named Apollos as being a learned man instructed in the way of the Lord and who had a thorough knowledge of the Scriptures. However, it disclosed that he was only familiar with the baptism of John. In verse twenty-six, Priscilla and Aquila invited him into their home "to explain the way of God more adequately." So, here is a believer who seemingly had all the components of being a Christian, having the knowledge of salvation, a baptism of repentance, and understanding of the Scriptures, but he was still pictured as having a void in some area of his faith. Although the actual topic of what was discussed is never disclosed, the verses that immediately follow expound on how Paul went to Ephesus and questioned the believers there if they received the baptism of the Holy Spirit.

Finally, in Acts 19:1-7, Paul asks some disciples if they received the Holy Spirit when they believed. When they answered negatively, he asked them what type of baptism they received. They answer John's baptism. With that, it says he placed hands on them and the Holy Spirit came upon them and they spoke in tongues and prophesied.

The apostles were instructed by Jesus to wait for their baptisms of the Spirit as revealed in Acts 1:4-5, "Do not leave Jerusalem, but wait for the gift my Father promised, which you have heard me speak about. For John baptized with water, but in a few days you will be baptized with the Holy Spirit." This command was given even though the apostles initially received the Spirit when Jesus breathed on them as spoken of in John 20:22. Prior to the day of Pentecost, the apostles were timid and were only interested in gaining power in Jesus' future kingdom. Peter at one point even denies that he knew Jesus. However, the apostles were transformed after their spiritual baptism. They began to boldly proclaim their faith, even to the point of willingly sacrificing their lives for their beliefs.

My spiritual baptism, in a similar manner, had a profound effect in my life. I desired to share the gospel and this experience with others. When I would tell others about this event, some would immediately reject it because it seemed so out of the ordinary. Others asked me if I thought they had salvation even though they were not baptized in the Spirit. I told them that nothing in Scripture indicated that it was necessary for salvation. Instead, I would tell them that it appears to be a "supercharging" of the Spirit within a believer allowing the Spirit to work through a person more powerfully, thus accomplishing much more for the kingdom of God. Lastly, a few asked me how they could receive this blessing. Usually, I encouraged them to find a Life in the Spirit seminar at a local Catholic church or to find a church whose doctrine supports spiritual baptism.

The question about how to receive a spiritual baptism made me curious though, so again I reexamined Scriptures in which a spiritual baptism occurred. I noticed that each baptism of the Spirit seemed to be unique whoever received it. It could be done by laying hands on someone, like how I received it. Sometimes it happened when people were gathered together listening to someone preach, such as when the apostles were assembled on the day of Pentecost. A man named Cornelius, his relatives, and his friends were also anointed with the Spirit as they listened to Peter preach as recorded in Acts 10:44. However, Paul (Saul) was filled with the Holy Spirit after a man named Ananias placed his hands upon him in Acts 9:17, indicating that it could be bestowed on a one-on-one basis. In any event, if anyone really yearns to have this gift, and if they pray sincerely for it, I believe that God will fashion events to have them receive it.

Whatever the specifics of a spiritual baptism are, one thing is for certain: whenever it occurs, the person who received it gains new boldness for Christ and his or her life changes forever. I believe that a spiritual baptism can be the next step for a Christian looking to go deeper if they have only had a baptism of repentance.

Scripture

Mark 1:4: And so John came, baptizing in the desert region and preaching a baptism of repentance for the forgiveness of sins.

Luke 7:30 But the Pharisees and experts in the law rejected God's purpose for themselves, because they had not been baptized by John.

Matthew 3:13-16: Then Jesus came from Galilee to the Jordan to be baptized by John. But John tried to deter him, saying, "I need to be baptized by you, and do you come to me?"

Jesus replied, "Let it be so now; it is proper for us to do this to fulfill all righteousness." Then John consented.

As soon as Jesus was baptized, he went up out of the water. At that moment heaven was opened, and he saw the Spirit of God descending like a dove and lighting on him.

Acts 1:4-5: On one occasion, while he was eating with them, he gave them this command: "Do not leave Jerusalem, but wait for the gift my Father promised, which you have heard me speak about. For John baptized with water, but in a few days you will be baptized with the Holy Spirit."

Acts 2:1-4: When the day of Pentecost came, they were all together in one place. Suddenly a sound like the blowing of a violent wind came from heaven and filled the whole house where they were sitting. They saw what seemed to be tongues of fire that separated and came to rest on each of them. All of them were filled with the Holy Spirit and began to speak in other tongues as the Spirit enabled them.

Matthew 3:11: "I baptize you with water for repentance. But after me comes one who is more powerful than I, whose sandals I am not fit to carry. He will baptize you with the Holy Spirit and fire."

Acts 8:14-16: When the apostles in Jerusalem heard that Samaria had accepted the word of God, they sent Peter and John to them. When they arrived, they prayed for them that they might receive the Holy Spirit, because the Holy Spirit had not yet come upon any of them; they had simply been baptized into the name of the Lord Jesus.

Acts 18:24-26: Meanwhile a Jew named Apollos, a native of Alexandria, came to Ephesus. He was a learned man, with a thorough knowledge of the Scriptures. He had been instructed in the way of the Lord, and he spoke with great fervor and taught about Jesus accurately, though he knew only the baptism of John. He began to speak boldly in the synagogue. When Priscilla and Aquila heard him, they invited him to their home and explained to him the way of God more adequately.

Acts 19:1-7:

While Apollos was at Corinth, Paul took the road through the interior and arrived at Ephesus. There he found some disciples and asked them, "Did you receive the Holy Spirit when you believed?" They answered, "No, we have not even heard that there is a Holy Spirit." So Paul asked, "Then what baptism did you receive?" "John's baptism," they replied. Paul said, "John's baptism was a baptism of repentance. He told the people to believe in the one coming after him, that is, in Jesus." On hearing this, they were baptized into the name of the Lord Jesus. When Paul placed his hands on them, the Holy Spirit came on them, and they spoke in tongues and prophesied. There were about twelve men in all.

Luke 11:13: "If you then, though you are evil, know how to give good gifts to your children, how much more will your Father in heaven give the Holy Spirit to those who ask him!"

—3—

Angels

M y husband David was very leery of my baptism in the Spirit experience. However, the Lord seemed to intervene a few days later to lay to rest any misgivings he had about the event.

David stopped at a store after work, and while there, some random man happened to strike up a conversation with him. Somehow they wandered onto the topic of my spiritual baptism. David confided to this man, "I'm not so sure that this baptism of the Spirit isn't some sort of deranged religious faction. Maybe Father Ken is somehow twisted."

"Oh, Father Ken—he's a good guy. I'm sure whatever happened is fine," the man assured David.

They continued to talk, my husband told me, and eventually the man asked David, "Do you have any children? Is your wife at home now?" When David responded that he did, the man gently encouraged, "You should go home to them."

Following the man's suggestion, David drove home and then disclosed to me the conversation he had just had with this man. After telling me the story, David declared, "I believe he may have been an angel. It was just so strange. He had a Slavic name. That really stood out to me." My husband had a Ukrainian heritage so the Slavic name was special to him. He continued, "It was odd that he asked me about you and the kids and then told me that I should go home. It's weird to tell another guy to just go home to his family."

David's story amazed me. I questioned if God had sent an angel to alleviate the fears my husband had about my baptism of the Spirit. I had previously read the book *Angels* by Billy Graham, which disclosed that angels are mentioned close to 300 times in both the Old and New Testaments.[1] Many of those times, they were interacting with humans in some capacity, so I knew that an angel visiting David was within the realm of possibility. This made me curious to learn more about these divine beings.

Therefore, I researched all the duties that angels fulfilled whenever they were recorded in the Word. Hebrews 1:14 identifies angels as "ministering spirits sent to serve those who will inherit salvation." Psalm 103:20 additionally revealed that they praise God and "do his bidding." That means that an angel could have certainly visited my husband if God wanted to validate my spiritual baptism to him. Another duty was proclaiming present and future events to mankind, such as when they announced to Mary about her becoming the mother of Jesus and informing the shepherds about Jesus' birth. Angels also carried out God's directive to exercise judgment upon the wicked, as portrayed in 1 Corinthians 10:10 that speak of a destroying angel.

Examining Hebrews 1:14 further, it refers to them as spirits. Yet, they apparently can materialize in a human form, as verified in Hebrews 13:2, which states, "Do not forget to entertain strangers, for by so doing some people have entertained angels without knowing it." Clearly, angels can take the form of strangers and interact with mankind.

Reflecting upon these revelations about angels, I mulled over David's encounter with this man. Why would this man and David get into a conversation about my being baptized with the Spirit of all topics? It amazed me that he would even be familiar with this practice as I never even heard of it prior to receiving it. He even approved of it, not thinking it was some invalid or out-dated practice for today. It was also strange that he knew Father Ken. Finally, what were the chances that this man having a Slavic name? Why had he even encouraged David to go home?

What astounded me the most though, was that David was moved to share this chance meeting with me and that he believed that the man was an angel. In any event, David no longer was suspicious of Father Ken or my baptism of the Spirit experience.

Scripture

Daniel 10:18: Again the one who looked like a man touched me and gave me strength.

Hebrews 13:2: Do not forget to entertain strangers, for by so doing some people have entertained angels without knowing it.

Hebrews 1:14: Are not all angels ministering spirits sent to serve those who will inherit salvation?

<u>**Tasks of Angels**</u>

Exodus 23:20 (Guarding people): "See, I am sending an angel ahead of you to guard you along the way and to bring you to the place I have prepared."

Psalm 103:20 (Carrying out God's directives): Praise the LORD, you his angels, you mighty ones who do his bidding, who obey his word.

Luke 2:13-14 (Praising God): Suddenly a great company of the heavenly host appeared with the angel, praising God and saying, "Glory to God in the highest, and on earth peace to men on whom his favor rests."

Acts 8:26 (Guiding people): Now an angel of the Lord said to Philip, "Go south to the road—the desert road—that goes down from Jerusalem to Gaza."

1 Corinthians 10:10 (Carrying out punishment): And do not grumble, as some of them did—and were killed by the destroying angel.

—4—

Demons

When I was a senior in college and working on my education degree at Penn State, I was assigned to do the final part of my student teaching. It was only to last for last six weeks of the ten-week term so I needed to find a place to live at school for the first four weeks. I came across a two-bedroom apartment that already had five girls living in it but who didn't mind having another person for that short of time. Although the conditions were cramped, I had a lot of fun as the girls were always up for doing something.

During this time, one of my roommates, Pam, suggested, "Let's drive to Pittsburgh and visit this teahouse I heard about where they tell your fortune!" I and another girl excitedly agreed to go there the following weekend. Not having strong Christian beliefs at the time, I wasn't as opposed to this practice as I would be today. Instead, I was intrigued that someone might actually possess the ability to reveal my future to me.

When that Saturday arrived, we made our way to the city and parked the car near where this place was located. After walking the rest of the way to the address, we found the doorway to the tearoom wedged between two businesses. As we passed through the door, we were faced with a steep staircase and proceeded to climb it. Upon reaching the top landing, we walked down a short, dark hallway and entered a room sprinkled with round tables. Most had several people sitting around them and a low murmur of chatter could be heard.

A woman came over and greeted us and then led us to one of the tables. We ordered tea and nervously talked as we waited for a spiritualist to make her way to us. It was not long before an ordinary-looking, middle-aged woman took the vacant seat at our table.

"Who wants to go first?" she questioned. Pam enthusiastically volunteered. The fortune-teller shuffled a set of tarot cards and sporadically laid one upon the table in front of her. Each time she did, she shared some insight about my friend's life. Pam confirmed that the woman's words were indeed related to her life and I was amazed.

When my turn arrived, the specificity of this woman's discernment shocked me. Her claims were not at all vague like I thought they would be. I was enthralled at her ability to identify issues occurring in my life at the time and for being able to forecast my future. I thought to myself, instead of just waiting for life to unfold, I had more control because I would know what to expect. I felt empowered and began thinking about when I could visit again. However, somewhere in my mind swirled the thought that this was terribly wrong, but I chose to ignore it.

I returned to the teahouse a couple of more times over the next few years. However, something occurred after my last visit that stopped my desire to ever want to go again. At the time, I was getting my master's degree and was sharing a two-bedroom apartment with another girl. After driving back from the teahouse one night, I settled into bed. Soon, I began to hear small, creaking noises. I had no idea what was causing them and just tried to relax. At first there were one or two and I thought they would end soon. But as I began to concentrate more and more upon them, they just became more frequent and louder, and began to really scare me.

My heart raced. I imagined demons were swirling about the room in the dark. The room continued to creak noisily and frequently, and I was terrified. I just froze in my bed and closed my eyes in fear. I tried to get some rest but sleep eluded me for most of the night.

When morning broke, the noises were gone but a feeling of uneasiness had now settled upon me. I felt like my visits to the teahouse had opened me up to this dark side of life. I sought protection from this uncomfortable feeling, so I paged through the telephone book to find the address of the nearest Catholic church. I thought a Godly atmosphere could relieve me of this oppression. I got dressed and immediately drove to the church that I looked up and went inside to seek comfort. However, surprisingly to me, this spiritual environment did not provide the relief I sought.

In the following weeks, an ever-present feeling of unrest continued to permeate my life. I made plans to visit my boyfriend, David, at Penn State University, hoping his presence would give me protection from this unrest. However, being with him did not ease the anxiety that began that night. Eventually, I finally found peace after attending a family reunion when I talked to my brother Richard. While there, I confessed to him, "I feel like things are chasing me, and nothing can protect me from them."

He replied, "Those powers cannot have power over you unless you let them. If you stand up to them, they will quit." Since nothing else seemed to be working, I took his advice and I refused to allow the uneasiness to overtake me. With time, the discomforting feelings lessened, then finally ceased. Regaining a sense of stability, I vowed to never again return to the teahouse.

I learned firsthand that there is an aspect of the spiritual world that is not related to God—the very real presence of demonic spirits. Ezekiel 28:12-18 and Isaiah 14:12-14 shed light on how this aspect of the world came into being. They uncover that Satan originally was one of God's most beautiful angels and was filled with great wisdom. However, Satan, because of these attributes, became prideful and wished to usurp God. He enlisted help from a third of the other angels and waged war against God and His army of the remaining angels. God, being all-powerful, banished him and these rebellious celestial beings from heaven and hurled them down to earth. Satan and the rejected angels, now known as demons, were then given some power to rule over the earth. In lieu of worshipping God, their mission is to try to derail as many people as possible through temptation and deception to pay homage to Satan. God allows this for the present but, at an appointed time, God will finally defeat him and his followers.

We do not need to fear Satan and his henchmen. James 4:7 and Matthew 4:10-11 illustrate that through

God's power we can command him to flee from us. Furthermore, by putting on the armor of God as outlined in Ephesians 6:11-17, we can protect ourselves from the devil and his temptations. Truth, righteousness, peace, faith, salvation, and the Spirit are our spiritual weapons we can employ against Satan.

It is only when we willingly yield to the lure of sin, such as seeking out spiritualists as condemned in Leviticus 19:31, that we permit these evil influences to have access into our lives. However, if we ever find that we have succumbed to the devil's deceits, we can always turn back to God and seek His help. He will make these spirits depart as God ultimately has power over everything in life.

Scripture

Ezekiel 28:12-18:

"Son of man, take up a lament concerning the king of Tyre and say to him: 'This is what the Sovereign LORD says:

"'You were the model of perfection,
    full of wisdom and perfect in beauty.
You were in Eden,
    the garden of God;
every precious stone adorned you:
    ruby, topaz and emerald,
    chrysolite, onyx and jasper,
    sapphire, turquoise and beryl.
Your settings and mountings were made of gold;

on the day you were created they were prepared.
You were anointed as a guardian cherub,
    for so I ordained you.
You were on the holy mount of God;
    you walked among the fiery stones.
You were blameless in your ways
    from the day you were created
    till wickedness was found in you.
Through your widespread trade
    you were filled with violence,
    and you sinned.
So I drove you in disgrace from the mount of God,
    and I expelled you, O guardian cherub,
    from among the fiery stones.
Your heart became proud
    on account of your beauty,
and you corrupted your wisdom
    because of your splendor.
So I threw you to the earth;
    I made a spectacle of you before kings.
By your many sins and dishonest trade
    you have desecrated your sanctuaries.
So I made a fire come out from you,
    and it consumed you,
and I reduced you to ashes on the ground
    in the sight of all who were watching.'"

Isaiah 14:12-14:
How you have fallen from heaven,
    O morning star, son of the dawn!
You have been cast down to the earth,
    you who once laid low the nations!
You said in your heart,

"I will ascend to heaven;
I will raise my throne
     above the stars of God;
I will sit enthroned on the mount of assembly,
     on the utmost heights of the sacred mountain.
I will ascend above the tops of the clouds;
     I will make myself like the Most High."

Ephesians 2:2: In which you used to live when you followed the ways of this world and of the ruler of the kingdom of the air, the spirit who is now at work in those who are disobedient.

Leviticus 19:31: "Do not turn to mediums or seek out spiritists, for you will be defiled by them. I am the LORD your God."

Leviticus 20:6: "I will set my face against the person who turns to mediums and spiritists to prostitute himself by following them, and I will cut him off from his people."

Ephesians 6:11-17:
     Put on the full armor of God so that you can take your stand against the devil's schemes. For our struggle is not against flesh and blood, but against the rulers, against the authorities, against the powers of this dark world and against the spiritual forces of evil in the heavenly realms. Therefore put on the full armor of God, so that when the day of evil comes, you may be able to stand your ground, and after you have done everything, to stand. Stand firm then, with the belt of truth buckled around your waist, with the

breastplate of righteousness in place, and with your feet fitted with the readiness that comes from the gospel of peace. In addition to all this, take up the shield of faith, with which you can extinguish all the flaming arrows of the evil one. Take the helmet of salvation and the sword of the Spirit, which is the word of God.

James 4:7b: "Resist the devil and he will flee from you."

Matthew 4:10-11: Jesus said to him, "Away from me, Satan! For it is written: 'Worship the Lord your God, and serve him only.'" Then the devil left him, and angels came and attended him.

—5—

Speaking in Tongues

"Try to move your tongue. Something in motion is easier to start than something stationary," encouraged our Life in the Spirit group leaders. It was our last meeting, and in an effort to help us grow in our spiritual walks, our mentors attempted to have us exercise the ability to speak in tongues. I didn't know what this meant at the time, but later discovered it was part of a larger set of abilities called the "Gifts of the Spirit" that one receives when baptized in the Spirit. These gifts are given to enable one to more effectively witness to others and to build up the church.[1]

Some Christians argue that they are actually given when someone accepts Christ, but in any event, being baptized with the Spirit seems to "supercharge" the person spiritually. First Corinthians 12:7-11 lists some of these abilities as being able to heal, perform miracles, prophesize, distinguish between spirits, speak in tongues, and interpret tongues. This is different from the "Fruits of the Spirit," which are what is produced when one follows the way of the Spirit. Galatians 5:22-23 lists those fruits as "Love, joy, peace, forbearance, kindness, goodness, faithfulness, gentleness and self-control."

Speaking in tongues, as I was to find out, is a divinely-driven prayer language. The resulting utterances are only understood by God and those whom God enables. It can be employed either privately or in a corporate setting and can emerge as words or be used in song. Because God forms the words, it is a very effective form of petition since it will always be in accordance with God's will and can be directed for things and situations of which the person may be unaware. Romans 8:26-27 possibly refers to this divine language when it states, "In the same way, the Spirit helps us in our weakness. We do not know what we ought to pray for, but the Spirit himself intercedes for us through wordless groans that words cannot express. And he who searches our hearts knows the mind of the Spirit, because the Spirit intercedes for the saints in accordance with God's will."

When employed in a corporate environment, it can be manifested as a message that gives revelation, knowledge, prophecy, or word of instruction. However, when used in such a manner, Scripture warns that it should be limited to just three people sharing and only allowed if there is an interpreter present. Otherwise, Scripture warns that it might evoke pride in the speaker and be unedifying to others.

Still not sure about this gift, I moved my tongue up and down as the instructors encouraged. To my surprise, eventually it seemed to move of its own accord. "Elee, lee, lee," came forth from my mouth. It did not overpower me. I could control it, similar to how one can start or stop singing. Although the sounds that I made were rudimentary, I was relieved that something materialized, as some people around me seemed unable to produce anything.

I observed later in Scripture that speaking in tongues seemed to accompany those who had been baptized with the Spirit, but then I reflected on those in my group who had no success. Maybe there was some area of sin in these people's lives that was blocking them from being able to speak in tongues or maybe they were too fearful or stubborn. Maybe it was given only to some people since 1 Corinthians 12:11 says that the Spirit gives as He determines.

I continued my experimentation as I drove home from the church, but my attempts reaped no more complexity. I concluded it must take practice to gain the more intricate sounds that I heard in church later that night when so many sang with such complexity. It sounded so beautiful and mystical that it made me picture what heaven would be like someday.

Years later when I tried to explain my experience with others in a different church, they immediately denied its existence for today. They argued that it was only employed to get the early church started. I didn't agree, as I had experienced it and had heard others using it. Additionally, I never saw any indications in the Bible that it was only for a certain time period in the church. Instead, I thought about the verse that cautioned us from adding to or subtracting from Scripture.

However, I understood how this gift could evoke emotions of fear because it of its mysteriousness. Even the early church seems to have struggled with this phenomenon. Paul, in 1 Corinthians 14, commanded that believers should not prohibit the speaking of tongues.

However, he prompted that it should not be prized above the other gifts.

I didn't dispute with my fellow church members too much because I felt inept at using the gift myself. I rarely attempted to speak in tongues myself as I never progressed beyond my initial, "Elee, lee, lee." However, I continued to be curious about the gift of tongues.

Out of chance one day, a friend of mine shared that she possessed an elementary level of speaking in tongues. However, after she read a book that said that tongues were for every believer who has been baptized with the Spirit, she was inspired to employ this gift more frequently. After doing so, she said that her tongues had gained more complexity. This encouraged me to try speaking in tongues again, but only on one occasion did I ever gain more depth.

A few months later, I was listening to a Christian television show and the preacher explained how using tongues will strengthen your connection to the Lord. He said by doing so, we also would receive more blessings in our lives. He offered the idea of exercising it while driving or in the shower.

From what I've witnessed during the Life in the Spirit seminars and from my own attempts, I believe that this gift is applicable to the Christian church today and that it should not be dismissed.

Scripture

Mark 16:17: And these signs will accompany those who believe: In my name they will drive out demons; they will speak in new tongues.

1 Corinthians 12:7-12:

> Now to each one the manifestation of the Spirit is given for the common good. To one there is given through the Spirit the message of wisdom, to another the message of knowledge by means of the same Spirit, to another faith by the same Spirit, to another gifts of healing by that one Spirit, to another miraculous powers, to another prophecy, to another distinguishing between spirits, to another speaking in different kinds of tongues, and to still another the interpretation of tongues. All these are the work of one and the same Spirit, and he gives them to each one, just as he determines.

Acts 2:4: All of them were filled with the Holy Spirit and began to speak in other tongues as the Spirit enabled them.

Acts 10:44-46a: While Peter was still speaking these words, the Holy Spirit came on all who heard the message. The circumcised believers who had come with Peter were astonished that the gift of the Holy Spirit had been poured out even on Gentiles. For they heard them speaking in tongues and praising God.

Acts 19:6: When Paul placed his hands on them, the Holy Spirit came on them, and they spoke in tongues and prophesied.

Romans 8:26-27: In the same way, the Spirit helps us in our weakness. We do not know what we ought to pray for, but the Spirit himself intercedes for us with groans that words cannot express. And he who searches our hearts knows the mind of the Spirit, because the Spirit intercedes for the saints in accordance with God's will.

1 Corinthians 14:6: Now, brothers, if I come to you and speak in tongues, what good will I be to you, unless I bring you some revelation or knowledge or prophecy or word of instruction?

1 Corinthians 14:14-15: For if I pray in a tongue, my spirit prays, but my mind is unfruitful. So what shall I do? I will pray with my spirit, but I will also pray with my mind; I will sing with my spirit, but I will also sing with my mind.

1 Corinthians 14: 18-19: I thank God that I speak in tongues more than all of you. But in the church I would rather speak five intelligible words to instruct others than ten thousand words in a tongue.

1 Corinthians 14:27-28: If anyone speaks in a tongue, two—or at the most three—should speak, one at a time, and someone must interpret. If there is no interpreter, the speaker should keep quiet in the church and speak to himself and God.

1 Corinthians 14:39: Therefore, my brothers, be eager to prophesy, and do not forbid speaking in tongues.

−6−

Understanding the Bible

I had always believed that the Bible was a special book. My parents had several sprinkled throughout our house and on several occasions, I had even cracked one open and scanned its pages. However, whenever I attempted to read it, it just seemed like a jumbled mess of words for me, too vague and mysterious to be helpful. Invariably, because of my difficulty in understanding it and not learning much from it, I would just put it back onto the shelf.

Years later when I was living in the Maple Ridge community of townhouses, I was encouraged to make an effort to examine the Bible again since so many of my neighbors in the cul-de-sac were Christians. I believed it had to be good for me even if I had little idea what I was reading. I resolved in my heart to read a chapter daily and did so every morning believing that it would give my day a firm foundation. Thus began my daily habit of reading scripture.

Three years later, the day after I was baptized with the Holy Spirit, I opened the Bible and began my reading as usual. This time it was different though. Something had changed; it suddenly was much more understandable. *"Why couldn't I understand this before?"* I wondered. My spiritual experience with the Holy Spirit seemed to have removed some barrier that had previously prevented me from understanding.

Eventually, I discovered passages in Scripture that actually validated the fact that the Bible is not understandable until you turn your heart over to the Lord. Second Corinthians 3:14-15 states that a veil exists whenever the old covenant or Moses is read, but whenever anyone turns to the Lord, the veil is removed. Second Corinthians 4:3-4 says that the gospel remains veiled to those who are perishing.

Now that the Bible was so much more understandable to me, I found it much more fascinating as I discovered many new insights. I continued my daily routine of reading until I had read the entire way through it. Then after accomplishing this, I chose to read another translation. This time, the thought came to me to write out summaries of each verse. I had heard that this was practiced by the leaders in the Bible Study Fellowship, a Christian women's organization. Therefore, I purchased a college-ruled notebook and, every day, attempted to summarize each verse that I read. I did this until I filled up one page. Over time, I gradually just turned to writing out each section word for word as that seemed easier to do. This method forced me to think about each verse much more closely.

Spending time in the Bible in this manner began to transform me. I liken it to how food nourishes our physical bodies. We are unaware how our bodies use the food we eat while we are eating it, but we notice how the food affects us overall. Likewise, when we read Scripture, we may not immediately be aware of its spiritual effect, but we are given a sense of direction in our spiritual walk and peace descends upon us. Isaiah 55:11 claims that, "My word that goes out from my mouth: It will not return to me empty, but will accomplish what I desire and achieve the purpose for which I sent it."

Immersing myself in His Word made me appreciate its uniqueness. It not only gives principles that promoted peaceful living in the present, but also is an accurate historical account of ancient times. Furthermore, it also reveals detailed predictions for the future.

Over time I began to learn more about the Bible. I found that it was authored by more than forty men on three different continents, in three different languages, and over a span of 1500 years. These men came from many different professions, including a king, a physician, a fisherman, a tax collector, a peasant, and a poet. Their writings had multiple styles—poems, songs, laws, parables, allegories, autobiographies, memoirs, and personal correspondences. Yet through all these differences, the main principles of God's plan for mankind remained the same.

Usually historic books attempt to sanitize the accounts of influential people, but the Bible presents these figures in an honest and straightforward manner. Both the righteousness and the shortcomings of people in the Bible are revealed. Noah got drunk, Moses murdered, Jacob swindled, David committed adultery, and Jonah ran away from his call from the Lord. Even Jesus' twelve disciples argued, displayed skepticism, and competed for glory.[1]

Furthermore, the Bible divulged some scientific facts long before they were widely accepted. Before the invention of the telescope in 1608 AD, scientists such as Ptolemy, Brahe, and Kepler estimated the stars in the sky to number to around a thousand or less. However, in the book of Jeremiah, believed to have been written before 600 B.C., records that the host of stars in the sky to be countless. The Bible even gives insights which man currently has no ability to fathom, such as the blueprint for the formation of the earth and the confinement of a man's life to one hundred and twenty years, which are outlined in the book of Genesis.[2]The Word described procedures for modern hygiene well before the knowledge that supported these practices was acquired. The Bible gives guidelines such as isolating sick people from others, destroying contaminated articles, burying fecal waste products, washing of hands, and abstaining from lifestyles that would encourage disease. Only in 1876 did Louis Pasteur and Robert Koch discover that germs propagated disease in people. Up to that point, common belief promoted that diseases spontaneously developed in a person from non-living substances.[3]

The Holy Scriptures contains an abundance of prophecies of which none have ever been discounted. The rise and destruction of nations and other political events have been foretold. Such events as the annihilation of Tyre and everlasting demise of Babylon were predicted many years before they happened and were given when these cities were thriving. The desecration of the temple and forthcoming rebuilding were revealed. A prophecy of more recent times told of return of the Jews to their own country of Israel. This happened in 1948.

In the end, it still requires faith to accept the Bible as being God's Word to mankind as there isn't definitive evidence to prove it. This same principle holds true for all the other tenets of Christianity, such as believing that Jesus is God's Son. This may be God's design though. If irrefutable evidence existed for these concepts, it would eliminate our freedom to choose, which is pivotal to Christianity.

Scripture

Isaiah 55:11: So is my word that goes out from my mouth: It will not return to me empty, but will accomplish what I desire and achieve the purpose for which I sent it.

Luke 24:45: Then he opened their minds so they could understand the Scriptures.

2 Corinthians 3:14-16: But their minds were made dull, for to this day the same veil remains when the old covenant is read. It has not been removed, because only in Christ is it taken away. Even to this day when Moses is read, a veil covers their hearts. But whenever anyone turns to the Lord, the veil is taken away.

2 Corinthians 4:3-4: "And even if our gospel is veiled, it is veiled to those who are perishing. The god of this age has blinded the minds of unbelievers, so that they cannot see the light of the gospel of the glory of Christ, who is the image of God."

2 Timothy 3:16-17: All Scripture is God-breathed and is useful for teaching, rebuking, correcting and training in righteousness, so that the man of God may be thoroughly equipped for every good work.

Hebrews 4:12: For the word of God is living and active. Sharper than any double-edged sword, it penetrates even to dividing soul and spirit, joints and marrow; it judges the thoughts and attitudes of the heart.

Knowledge given in the Bible

Genesis 1:1 (through verse 31): In the beginning God created the heavens and the earth...

Genesis 6:3 (Lifespan of man): Then the LORD said, "My Spirit will not contend with man forever, for he is mortal; his days will be a hundred and twenty years."

Leviticus 13:46 (Isolating the sick): As long as he has the infection he remains unclean. He must live alone; he must live outside the camp.

Leviticus 13:47-52 (Burning contaminated clothing): "If any clothing is contaminated with mildew — any woolen or linen clothing, any woven or knitted material of linen or wool, any leather or anything made of leather — and if the contamination in the clothing, or leather, or woven or knitted material, or any leather article, is greenish or reddish, it is a spreading mildew and must be shown to the priest. The priest is to examine the mildew and isolate the affected article for seven days. On the seventh day he is to examine it, and if the mildew has spread in the clothing, or the woven or knitted material, or the leather, whatever its use, it is a destructive mildew; the article is unclean. He must burn up the clothing, or the woven or knitted material of wool or linen, or any leather article that has the contamination in it, because the mildew is destructive; the article must be burned up.

Leviticus 14:9b (Washing hands and taking a bath): He must wash his clothes and bathe himself with water, and he will be clean.

Leviticus 20:13 (Against lifestyle that causes disease): If a man lies with a man as one lies with a woman, both of them have done what is detestable. They must be put to death; their blood will be on their own heads.

Deuteronomy 23:12-13 (Covering up waste): Designate a place outside the camp where you can go to relieve yourself. As part of your equipment have something to dig with, and when you relieve yourself, dig a hole and cover up your excrement.

Jeremiah 33:22 (Vast number of stars): I will make the descendants of David my servant and the Levites who minister before me as countless as the stars of the sky and as measureless as the sand on the seashore.

—7—

Giving Over Control

The snow was steadily coming down, and all the roads were becoming blanketed with snow quickly. I was a junior in college at the time and was driving across town in my 1974 Volkswagen Beetle to see some friends. I was my early twenties and was not very concerned about the dangerous driving conditions. I just wanted something to do that night instead of staying at home.

As my car approached a rather steep hill, I observed the car in front of me struggle to get up hill. It would start to ascend only to stop as it wheels couldn't find traction. I waited patiently and watched as it tried again but failed. However, on the third attempt, the vehicle finally started to ascend the slope. I could definitely tell that the roads were slippery from the snow. I proceeded to gently press on my accelerator to go up the hill myself. I aimed for the tire tracks of the previous car and was able to climb up without a problem. After cresting the hill, I slowly made my half-mile descent downward toward the interstate hoping it would be less snow covered than the back roads. When I reaching the on-ramp, I found this major highway was also very snow covered. I continued to drive slowly, attempting to be cautious, and thankfully made it to where I needed to exit. As I approached the off-ramp, I put my foot on the brake to negotiate the upcoming right turn. However, instead of slowing down, the slippery conditions made my car spin to the right. Out front window I could see I was aligned to plow into a quickly approaching guard rail!

I panicked and pressed the brake harder and harder thinking it might somehow catch grip. *Please stop!* Yet, my car did not respond at all and guard rail was quickly coming. Realizing that my struggling was not helping and that there was nothing else I could do, I gave up my efforts and thought to myself, *"Oh, well, I'm just going to crash..."*

Immediately after I gave up control, my car jerked to the left on its own, away from the rail, and cruised smoothly down the exit ramp. *"What just happened?"* I wondered to myself in amazement.

I sat there for a second in disbelief trying to figure out why my car jumped so dramatically to align itself down the exit ramp. I had no possible explanation in my mind. I continued on my way thankful that I had not crashed.

Later, I asked others I knew if there was a reason that my car could have straightened out so strangely. Maybe taking my foot off the brake caused my car to straighten out or something. Yet, no one I talked to about it seemed to have an explanation why my car would suddenly shift its direction perfectly. It made me wonder if one of God's angels had intervened and directed the car away from the guardrail.

Years later, I learned that God sometimes will not intercede in our problems until we stop relying on ourselves and give up control of the situation. I had read about several instances of God waiting to intervene in a situation until the person stopped trying to work things out on their own. The first was when someone who wanted to get married had tried every way possible to meet a spouse but had no luck. Then, when she came to peace with being single, she met the love of his life. The second example was when someone prayed so hard for a new job and worked tirelessly sending out resumes. After that yielded no results, he then prayed that he would content in his present job if that was what God wanted for him. Immediately a more desirable opportunity was presented to him.

I then remembered the driving experience from my junior year of college and how strange it had been that when I stopped trying to control the car, it snapped perfectly to the straight position. My experience with my car behaving in such an extraordinary manner led me to believe that God works most powerfully when we give up control and leave the results to Him.

Scripture

Proverbs 28:26: "He who trusts in himself is a fool, but he who walks in wisdom is kept safe."

2 Corinthians 12:10: That is why, for Christ's sake, I delight in weaknesses, in insults, in hardships, in persecutions, in difficulties. For when I am weak, then I am strong.

—8—

Submission

S hortly after I was baptized in the Spirit, Wilma, a woman who was involved in the Life in the Spirit Seminar, approached me to help her start a Mothers of Preschoolers group at Saint Steven's. I agreed and became the teaching coordinator shortly after. I kept that position for several years and, during those years, it was my responsibility to convey spiritual principles to the mothers in the group. This organization suggested a four-year cycle of lessons pertaining to womanhood, marriage, raising children, and issues concerning running a home. During the year that I taught about being a wife, I myself learned many Biblical precepts about what a Christian marriage should be.

One principle that I uncovered was on submission. In Ephesians 5:21-30, the Bible says, "Submit to one another out of reverence for Christ. Wives, submit to your husbands as to the Lord. For the husband is the head of the wife as Christ is the head of the church, his body, of which he is the Savior. Now as the church submits to Christ, so also wives should submit to their husbands in everything. Husbands, love your wives, just as Christ loved the church and gave himself up for her to make her holy, cleansing her by the washing with water through the word, and to present her to himself as a radiant church, without stain or wrinkle or any other blemish, but holy and blameless. In this same way, husbands ought to love their wives as their own bodies. He who loves his wife loves himself. After all, no one ever hated their own body, but he feeds and cares for it, just as Christ does the church—for we are members of his body."

I understood that many women took offense to this idea of submission, but it never really bothered me. I figured if a man was in favor of me looking towards him for leadership, then he should be willing to follow to the subsequent verses where he was commanded to love me as himself. Maybe this verse didn't scare me because I felt my husband would treat me fairly.

Years later, I also became familiar the concept that there are many negative consequences of opposing those in authority over us. Romans 13:1-2 claims that no authority is in existence except that which God has established. If anyone rebels against that authority, they actually are rebelling against God.

However, it was after reading the book, *Authority and Submission* by Watchman Nee that I gained further clarification about this topic. He proposed, "In the universe there are two great things: believing unto salvation and submitting to authority.[1]

In regards to authority, Nee continues and says that in any situation, we should reflect upon who has authority over us and to submit to that person. He states that whoever was created first and the person who has been saved the longest are to be over those who are younger and have known salvation the least amount of time.[2] Ephesians 6 also clarifies that children are to obey their parents, and slaves (employees) should listen to their masters (employers).

Jesus additionally confirmed that those in civic positions should be honored. Jesus showed this in Matthew 22:15-22 when the Pharisees were attempting to trap him with questions about paying taxes. When they asked if they were bound to such a practice, Jesus called them hypocrites and asked them whose image was on the coin. When they replied "Caesar's," he responded, "So give back to Caesar what is Caesar's, and to God what is God's."

Nee went on and declared that failing to adhere to this directive of humbling oneself is a very serious sin and can cause one to face severe consequences. He cited a few examples where God punished those who failed to respect authority. One occurred when Noah got drunk after exiting the ark. Although this behavior was not praiseworthy, Ham, Noah's son, acted dishonorably toward his father. When he discovered his father passed out and naked, he didn't have any shame or sorrow. Instead, he gazed upon him and then shared his father's disgrace with his two brothers. After Noah awoke, he prophesied that Ham would be cursed and become a servant to his brothers. On the other hand, his other two brothers refused to look at their father and covered him up. They were blessed as Jesus was born out of Shem's bloodline and Japheth's descendants were destined to preach about Christ.[3]

Another illustration given was how God looked unfavorably upon Miriam when she disrespected her brother

Moses, even though he had been anointed by God. In Numbers 12:2 she charges, "Has the LORD spoken only through Moses? Hasn't he also spoken through us?" When Miriam overstepped her position, God immediately struck Miriam with leprosy.[4]

It is interesting how Moses responded to this attack. Instead of reminding Miriam that God had chosen him, he says nothing. Scripture just states that Moses was a very humble man and depended upon the Lord to defend his position. Instead, Moses prays for Miriam to be healed of this dreaded disease.[5] Nee observes that all those in a position of authority should react in a like manner.[6]

David, also ordained by God for leadership, never tried to secure that position through his own might. Instead, he honored Saul as king and waited upon the Lord to secure the throne in His own time. Even when presented with several opportunities to kill Saul and take his throne, he refrained from doing so. When an Amalekite informed David that he slew Saul, David responded in 2 Samuel 1:14, "Why were you not afraid to lift your hand to destroy the LORD's anointed?" Then in verse 15 it says, "Then David called one of his men and said, "Go, strike him down!" So he struck him down, and he died." David truly took the principle of submission seriously![7]

Even if the person in authority does not appear worthy of their leadership, honor is still demanded. This can arise when the person in charge is instructing others to do things that oppose God's instructions. In such cases, we may refrain from following their wrong commands, but we must maintain humility and an attitude of respect toward the misguided superior.

Nee pointed out several times in Scripture where this occurred. One was when the Israelite midwives and Moses' mother spared the Israelites babies against Pharaoh's order to kill them. Another incidence was when Daniel continued to worship God, even though King Nebuchadnezzar gave the order for everyone to only glorify his golden image. In both of these cases, although they failed to follow the decrees, they did not contemptuously rebel. In their heart and words, they still had a spirit of reverence for those over them.[8]

In any event, all of creation falls under this principle of submission, even wives to their husbands. The way I tried to follow this spiritual rule was simple. The first way was by being very open with my husband in all things. If I found myself disagreeing over something that my husband felt was best for our family, I presented my opinion respectfully. But then I let him know I that I would comply with whatever he thought. Shockingly, by doing so, I found that my husband more readily listened to my thoughts. He wanted to be fair since the responsibility for the final decision rest with him.

When the time came for David and me to buy a house, I continued to be submissive to his choice in a home. After searching for houses for nearly two years, I found one particular home that I thought suited our needs well. It was selling at a price much lower than the surrounding homes and was in a pleasant neighborhood where our children could find playmates. It was only eight years old, had four bedrooms, and offered a great mortgage option. I strongly encouraged David that we should make an offer, but he was hesitant. He wanted more privacy than this house offered since was on a quarter acre lot and had houses to the left, right, and rear of it. Although

I told David I would go along with whatever he decided, I cautioned him that another house like this might not come along again for a long time. He mulled it over and eventually agreed with me.

Shortly after moving in, however, David started to grumble about it. Even though David ultimately had chosen to purchase this house, I knew I had sort of pressured him and had not really considered his preferences. It didn't take long until we began to search for another house with more acreage and more seclusion. Part of me thought that it really was more for entertainment's sake since we did not want to spend more than what we had spent on our current home.

We remained in our house, but for the next couple years, we spent many weekends looking at other properties. Finally, we decided to tour one particular house that was in an adjacent community. David liked the large plot of land and the wooded area bordering the back side. After viewing the interior of the house, David turned to me and excitedly asked, "What do you think of this place?"

Although the location and yard were nice, the house, where I would be spending most of my time, was not what I would have selected. Since I felt like I had almost forced David into buying our first house and he was discontent with it, I wanted him chose where we lived now. I replied, "If you like it, let's get it.""Could you work up some numbers for us?" David asked as he turned to the agent. After reviewing the costs, and with my approval, he excitedly told her that we'd like to make an offer.

An agreement was reached, so we put our current home up for sale. We listed with a low asking price so that we could move quickly since our next child was due in four months. However, weeks went by without any offers on our home. I thought that the unflattering décor, which we hadn't had time or money to change, probably deterred prospective buyers. David became anxious, so we lowered our price even more.

"I don't understand why this house isn't selling. It is such a great bargain," a seasoned real estate agent who was showing our house commented. "I'm determined to get you a buyer," she said.

Our house continued to sit on the market for nearly two months. Then one night, David and I were sitting in our living room listening to the radio. "People who live in homes close to large power lines risk a greater chance of contracting cancer," the broadcaster shared. David's ears perked up. The house we were considering was located pretty close to a rather large high-voltage line. The more David listened, the more concerned he became.

"I don't want to buy that house now. Our agreement is dependent upon our selling our house, and since we haven't been able to sell it, maybe they will just let us out of it," he suggested.

"I don't know. We still have two more weeks left," I reminded him.

"Just call and see what they say," he urged.

"Okay," I agreed. I figured that when I called, I could say that I had thought our house would move more quickly, and now that I was closer to the due date of the baby, I was concerned about the difficulty of moving.

I telephoned our real estate agent the next day and asked her about terminating our contract immediately. She said she did not have a problem with that, but she would have to obtain permission from the listing agent of the house on which we had made an offer. She called back that afternoon and shared that the listing agent was not as agreeable.

That night our oldest child, Anna, got sick and kept me up most of the night. By morning I was exhausted, especially with the extra strain of being pregnant. When Anna finally settled down and fell asleep, I tried to slip back into bed to get some rest. Not long after I dozed off, the phone rang.

"Hel-lo," I croaked when I answered the phone, not fully being awake.

It was the listing agent for the other house. "I'd like to show your house today," she said.

My broken voice continued, "I just can't show it today. I was up all night with one of my children."

"Are you sure I can't show it?" she pressed.

"Sorry, but not today," I firmly replied.

The woman must have thought I was going to be difficult, because that next evening our real estate agent called and informed us that we had been released from the contract. My weary voice and refusal to show the house must have swayed the other agent's initial hesitancy to release us.

About a month later, David and I drove by the house we had almost purchased. Back by the woods was a huge bulldozer, and it looked as though a foundation for a new home was being excavated. That may have been why the owners of the house had originally put their home up for sale. Had we bought the house, we would not have had the privacy that attracted David to it in the first place.

I sometimes think back to this chain of events. It seemed odd how our house wasn't selling with such a low price. By chance, we heard about the danger of electrical wires. Then, Anna kept me up all night, so I had declined showing our house. All of this led to our getting out of the contract early. I personally felt that God rewarded my willingness to go along with my husband's desires over my own by helping us avoid purchasing a home that would not have pleased either David or me. David never complained about our home again.

Scripture

Romans 13:1-2: Everyone must submit himself to the governing authorities, for there is no authority except that which God has established. The authorities that exist have been established by God. Consequently, he who rebels against the authority is rebelling against what God has instituted, and those who do so will bring judgment on themselves.

Numbers 12:1-2, 13-14: Miriam and Aaron began to talk against Moses because of his Cushite wife, for he had married a Cushite. "Has the LORD spoken only through Moses?" they asked. "Hasn't he also spoken through us?" And the LORD heard this.

So Moses cried out to the LORD, "O God, please heal her!"

The LORD replied to Moses, "If her father had spit in her face, would she not have been in disgrace for seven days? Confine her outside the camp for seven days; after that she can be brought back."

2 Samuel 1:14-15: David asked him, "Why were you not afraid to lift your hand to destroy the LORD's anointed?"

Then David called one of his men and said, "Go, strike him down!" So he struck him down, and he died.

Philippians 2:5-8: Your attitude should be the same as that of Christ Jesus: Who, being in very nature God, did not consider equality with God something to be grasped, but made himself nothing, taking the very nature of a servant, being made in human likeness. And being found in appearance as a man, he humbled himself and became obedient to death—even death on a cross!

Hebrews 13:17: Obey your leaders and submit to their authority. They keep watch over you as men who must give an account. Obey them so that their work will be a joy, not a burden, for that would be of no advantage to you.

1 Peter 2:13: Submit yourselves for the Lord's sake to every authority instituted among men: whether to the king, as the supreme authority.

1 Peter 5:5: Young men, in the same way be submissive to those who are older. All of you, clothe yourselves with humility toward one another, because, "God opposes the proud but gives grace to the humble."

Colossians 3:18: Wives, submit to your husbands, as is fitting in the Lord.

1 Peter 3:1-2: Wives, in the same way submit yourselves to your husbands so that, if any of them do not believe the word, they may be won over without words by the behavior of their wives, when they see the purity and reverence of your lives.

1 Peter 3:5: For this is the way the holy women of the past who put their hope in God used to make themselves beautiful. They were submissive to their own husbands.

Ephesians 5:21-29:

Submit to one another out of reverence for Christ.

Wives, submit to your husbands as to the Lord. For the husband is the head of the wife as Christ is the head of the church, his body, of which he is the Savior. Now as the church submits to Christ, so also wives should submit to their husbands in everything.

Husbands, love your wives, just as Christ loved the church and gave himself up for her to make her holy, cleansing her by the washing with water through the word, and to present her to himself as a radiant church, without stain or wrinkle or any other blemish, but holy and blameless. In this same way, husbands ought to love their wives as their own bodies. He who loves his wife loves himself. After all, no one ever hated his own body, but he feeds and cares for it, just as Christ does the church.

Ephesians 6:1-9:

Children, obey your parents in the Lord, for this is right. "Honor your father and mother"—which is the first commandment with a promise—"that it may go well with you and that you may enjoy long life on the earth."

Fathers, do not exasperate your children; instead, bring them up in the training and instruction of the Lord.

Slaves, obey your earthly masters with respect and fear, and with sincerity of heart, just as you would obey Christ. Obey them not only to win their favor when their eye is on you, but like slaves of Christ, doing the will of God from your heart. Serve wholeheartedly, as if you were serving the Lord, not men, because you know that the Lord will reward everyone for whatever good he does, whether he is slave or free.

And masters, treat your slaves in the same way. Do not threaten them, since you know that he who is both their Master and yours is in heaven, and there is no favoritism with him.

—9—

Confessing Sins

When my first two children, Anna and Peter, were three and four, I got a call from a woman I had met the previous year in a group called "Mothers of Preschoolers." Her name was Jeanne and she asked me, "Would you like to join "Moms in Touch? It is a group where mothers gather together and pray for the schools and our children in them." She went on to inform me that Mary from the Maple Ridge townhouse community where my husband and I had lived, and her friend Ruth, had already committed.

It was a scary thought that I would have to send my children into the public school system in the very near future. Hopefully, our prayers would counter any negative influences they might face. I told her that I would love to join.

We met up at a Christian and a Missionary Alliance church that was not very far from my house. Jeanne's husband was a pastor and knew the minister of this church, who agreed that we could use its library to pray.

I was even able to bring Anna and Peter, who were happy to play in the toy-filled nursery room next door.

Jeanne had a background in teaching and efficiently directed our time together. She encouraged us to use a pattern of prayer that used the acronym A.C.T.S. The letters represented adoration, confession, thanksgiving, and supplication. Supplication-type prayers were the easiest. We just asked our heavenly Father for certain favors. Adoration and thanksgiving prayers were not difficult, but I wasn't used to them as much. Then there was confession. *Did I really want to expose my shortcomings to these women?*

As a Catholic, I was accustomed to telling my sins to a priest, who surely would understand that I was not perfect and was sworn to secrecy about them. But James 5:16 instructs believers to share their transgressions with other Christians. This seemed much more difficult than sharing them with a priest. I felt people would judge me if I didn't promote the idea that I had it all together.

As we continued to meet and everyone revealed more and more of their inability to be a perfect Christian, I felt safe to share my own shortcomings. It was embarrassing and difficult at first though. I was often selfish, prideful, cranky with the kids, and disrespectful to my husband.

Regularly exposing our failings to each other, I hated to admit, began to reap some benefits. Hearing others' struggles encouraged me because I realized that I was not alone in falling short of the glory of God. It deterred me from continuing to commit these transgressions in the upcoming week, since I knew I would have to reveal them the next time we met. It also refreshed me and gave me a new opportunity to try again to act in ways pleasing to our Lord.

An unexpected benefit from this practice was that it brought all of us women very close together. Seeing one another more honestly created solid bonds of friendship. To this day, whenever any major event happens in our lives, we know that we can rely on the others for prayer and support. Over the years, we have bathed many things in prayer including births, deaths, weddings, an organ transplant, cancer, a serious car accident, relationship difficulties, and employment struggles. I do not think we would ever have developed such strong ties with these women without first learning to humble ourselves by exposing our weaknesses before one another.

Scripture

James 5:16: "Therefore confess your sins to each other and pray for each other so that you may be healed. The prayer of a righteous man is powerful and effective."

1 John 1:9-10: If we confess our sins, he is faithful and just and will forgive us our sins and purify us from all unrighteousness. If we claim we have not sinned, we make him out to be a liar and his word has no place in our lives.

10

Prayer of Petition: One

It was the early eighties, and a less-than-stellar economy meant there were few job opportunities for my husband, David. After some time of job-hunting, he was offered employment as an engineer designing barges. However, because of continuing poor economic conditions, it was not long until company lay-offs left him jobless again. A few months later, he secured another engineering job, but it was not in his specialty of heavy duty machinery. Finally, after the recession ended, he was thrilled to obtain a job with a company that created and manufactured mill equipment.

Although happy to finally be designing larger projects, David soon felt underutilized at his job. He believed that he was being underpaid compared to other engineers and being passed over for working on the more challenging projects. He felt his boss at this new company was somehow prejudiced against him.

I knew David was intelligent and gifted in his field, and I hated to see his talents not being fully applied. I resorted to praying for David's work situation, knowing that I was helpless to make things better for him any other way.

Scripture is full of instructions to pray. Even Jesus, the Son of God, is portrayed as frequently praying. If our Lord found it necessary to petition God the Father, then certainly I should also. Therefore, for David's situation with his boss, I offered up a plea to God in an effort to have God intervene. The Lord was quick to answer my prayer. David returned home from work and informed me that his boss had decided to take a job elsewhere. David expressed his excitement that he would get to prove his talents to a new manager.

After he attended the farewell dinner for his departing boss, David came home and shared with me an odd remark that this man made during his parting speech. His former boss had said, "I really don't know why I am quitting. I love my job here." Since this was such a bizarre thing to say, it made us believe that it was a sign that the Lord had induced him to leave.

Under his new supervisor, David was soon assigned more demanding projects and his pay was increased significantly. This made him much more satisfied with his job.

The Word reveals that sometimes God chooses not intervene with the activities of mankind unless prayers are offered. Mark 9:25-29 tells of a man who had a son who was demon possessed. The disciples tried to release the boy from this bondage but failed. When they inquired of Jesus for the reason why, He replied, "This kind can come out only by prayer."

Also, in Job 42 God directs Job to make a burnt offering and specifically to pray for his three friends,

Eliphaz, Bildad, and Zophar. God was angry with them because they had incorrectly spoken about Him. Being a supreme being, you would think that He would just say that these men were forgiven. Instead, He directed Job to pray for their forgiveness.

This occurrence with David's boss leaving helped confirm my thought that when we face struggles in our life, we should turn to God in prayer. Although God cares about us, often He will wait until we look to Him to help us. In any case, I believe that the Lord intervened and prompted David's boss to leave, enabling David to better utilize his skills and feel better about himself.

Scripture

Colossians 4:2: Devote yourselves to prayer, being watchful and thankful.

1 Timothy 2:8: I want the men everywhere to lift up holy hands in prayer, without anger or disputing.

James 1:5: If any of you lacks wisdom, he should ask God, who gives generously to all without finding fault, and it will be given to him.

God Not Intervening Until Prayer is Offered

Job 42:7-8: After the LORD had said these things to Job, he said to Eliphaz the Temanite, "I am angry with you and your two friends, because you have not spoken what is right, as my servant Job has. So now take seven bulls and seven rams and go to my servant Job and sacrifice a burnt offering for yourselves. My servant Job will pray for you, and I will accept his prayer and not deal with you according to your folly. You have not spoken what is right, as my servant Job has."

Ezekiel 22:30-31: "I looked for a man among them who would build up the wall and stand before me in the gap on behalf of the land so I would not have to destroy it, but I found none. So I will pour out my wrath on them and consume them with my fiery anger, bringing down on their own heads all they have done, declares the Sovereign Lord."

Mark 9:25-29:

When Jesus saw that a crowd was running to the scene, he rebuked the evil spirit. "You deaf and mute spirit," he said, "I command you, come out of him and never enter him again."

The spirit shrieked, convulsed him violently and came out. The boy looked so much like a corpse that many said, "He's dead." But Jesus took him by the hand and lifted him to his feet, and he stood up.After Jesus had gone indoors, his disciples asked him privately, "Why couldn't we drive it out?"He replied, "This kind can come out only by prayer."

11

Prayer of Petition: Two

I was pregnant with my fourth child and about a week past my due date. As my obstetrician examined me, he stated, "You are ready to deliver this baby. I think we should induce you. Do you want to come back later today or do you want to wait until tomorrow?"

"Let's hold off until tomorrow," I replied, thinking that the next day's date of July 25 would be a more memorable birth date because it is sometimes referred to as Christmas in July. I also wanted to give the baby another day to see if he would come on his own.

By the next morning, however, I still didn't have any signs of labor, so David and I got ready and drove through the pre-morning rush-hour traffic to the hospital. I was admitted and brought into the labor room, where my gynecologist's associate performed a preliminary exam. "I'll start you on Pitocin, and then, by the time that kicks in, Dr. Saltsman should be here for the delivery. He's parking his car right now," he reported.

I received this labor-inducing drug through an IV, but it didn't seem to be having an effect. Nurses kept checking me, but I showed no signs of going into labor. Then suddenly, strong, swift pains materialized out of nowhere. In the deliveries of my other three children, I had utilized Lamaze, a breathing technique used to distract one from child birthing pains. However, this pain was so intense that I had a difficult time trying to use it now. All I could think to do was to cry out, "Lord, take this pain away!"

Immediately, all feelings of discomfort stopped and I relaxed. The pain had subsided so rapidly that I assumed the baby had already arrived. "Honey, you have to keep pushing," the nurse gently encouraged. Her words surprised me and I came back to reality. *Did God actually answer my prayer so instantly?* I continued with the birthing process, and amazingly, it continued to be pain-free.

In a short time, my fourth child and third baby boy was born. He came so quickly that Dr. Saltsman did not even have time to come in and deliver the newest addition to my family, Paul.

I never experienced anything like that in any of my other children's births. It was so incredible that I had such intense pains in the beginning that instantly went away when I called out to the Lord. In any case, I regretted that I had not sought the Lord's help during my other three children's births!

Scripture

Matthew 21:22: "If you believe, you will receive whatever you ask for in prayer."

Romans 12:12: Be joyful in hope, patient in affliction, faithful in prayer.

1 Thessalonians 5:16-18: Rejoice always, pray continually, give thanks in all circumstances; for this is God's will for you in Christ Jesus.

12

Prayer of Petition: Three

David came home from work one night with what he thought was a wonderful idea for the family. "Let's go camping," he suggested. "Someone gave me this booklet called 'Little-Known State Parks of Pennsylvania.' I'd like to take off a few days and go explore a few of them," he excitedly promoted.

To David, camping meant sleeping in a tent with no or very few facilities around. I normally enjoyed camping as a family, but we now had four kids aged two to ten, with the youngest two children in diapers. Life was a bit overwhelming to me at this point and I did not have energy to organize such a venture. "It's difficult enough to get through a regular day, David," I admitted. "However, I'll go, if you can get everything ready and shop for the food," I conceded.

"Sure. I can do that," David quickly agreed.

True to his word, he diligently prepared for our trip. David piled the camping supplies in our late model Ford Taurus wagon: two tents, six sleeping bags with pads, cooking utensils, fire-making equipment, clothes, a portable potty for our children, and an abundance of food. When everything was prepared, we packed into the car and hit the road.

We had left a bit later in the day since we never seemed to be able to get out of the house early. We cruised on the Interstate toward the Allegheny National Forest. Our first destination was a campground called Red Bridge, located near the Kinzua Dam. Leaving so late proved to be a mistake, as we arrived around ten o'clock at night. Stumbling through the darkness, we managed to set up the tent and get everyone's sleeping bags out of the car. Soon, everyone was fast asleep.

We were going to visit a lot of the campsites so the next morning, after cooking our breakfast over a fire, we packed our things back into the car and headed toward Prouty Place State Park. It was one of the less-visited parks in the guide, which meant it was very remote. The park ranger seemed quite surprised to see us and, probably being lonely, talked with David for some time. He revealed that the last visitors here had encountered a bear. Unruffled, David set up both tents while I watched our kids play by the nearby creek. We later feasted upon a dinner of chicken grilled over a campfire and enjoyed the beautiful scenery. So far we were enjoying our adventure into the wilderness.

The following day, we once again loaded our equipment into our car and then headed to the "Little Grand Canyon" of Pennsylvania. We had never been there before and the view was quite breath-taking. We admired the canyon for a little while before heading onward to Bald Eagle State Park to set up camp for the night. We discovered a wonderful site, nestled among lush trees.

There were abundant monkey vines, which provided great entertainment for our children as they swung to and fro on them. After dinner, our family talked around the campfire for a while before dozing off in our tents.

By the next morning, we had grown weary of living so primitively. It had been a nice trip so far, but cooking over a fire, sleeping on the hard ground, and not being able to take showers had all grown tiresome, so we decided to head home. As we were driving, John and Paul fell asleep, as it was now getting to be nighttime.

Around ten o'clock, we reached Cresson, Pennsylvania. This small town along the way was in the middle of the state and had a mountain that locals nicknamed "Little Alaska." This was because it had such a steep altitude that the weather at the top could be arctic in the wintertime because of its height. To get back home, we had to take the road that went up this steep incline. When we were approximately three-fourths of the way up this mountain, our car suddenly died. I was concerned. *Who in the world is going to help us? It is Friday night and no car repair shop is going to be opened. There aren't any businesses around, it is dark, and there isn't that much traffic.* Then I reasoned that we had camping gear in the car and could just camp on the side of the road if we had to do so.

Just after thinking this, a lightning bolt flashed ominously across the sky, followed by a huge thunderclap. *So much for that idea.* Paul, who had been quietly sleeping on my lap, was startled awake and immediately began to wail. That set John off, who had been sleeping in the backseat. Things were quickly turning bad. "Start praying," I suggested to my two older kids and David. So we prayed that God would intervene in this predicament.

In what seemed like just a few moments, a pair of headlights appeared right behind our car. The driver of the vehicle jumped out and approached David's window. "Do you need some help?" he asked.

"Yes, as a matter of fact, we do. Our car just stopped working," David replied.

"Get your family and come into our car," the man encouraged, gesturing to his large station wagon. "We'll have enough room for everyone." Figuring that we had no other option and that the man seemed nice enough, all six of us exited our car and amazingly managed to fit into his station wagon with his family. "Let's drop off your wife and children at a hotel. Then you and I can drive back to get your car and tow it to my house," the man further offered.

So he delivered the kids and me to a local hotel and then he and David headed back to our car. After getting it to his house, he drove David back to the hotel. Early the next morning, the man returned to the hotel to pick up David and take him back to the car, which was still at his house.

David was pretty knowledgeable about cars so after examining the vehicle, the man drove him to the auto parts store where David bought the necessary items. They then returned to the man's house and David proceeded to repair our car. In the meantime, checkout time at the hotel was drawing near, so the man returned to pick up the kids and me and gratuitously brought us to his house. About an hour later David had our car running, so we bid this kind family good-bye. We drove off thankful for their generosity and arrived home later that day without further incident.

In Scripture, God encourages us to pray when we are in trouble. I was so thankful that we did and amazed at how quickly and fully our prayers were answered in this situation. It made me wonder how many times I had faced difficulties in the past and would have suffered less if I had just turned to God for help.

Scripture

Philippians 4:6: Do not be anxious about anything, but in everything, by prayer and petition, with thanksgiving, present your requests to God.

James 5:13a: Is anyone among you in trouble? He should pray.

—13—

Life after Death

"**D**avid has passed away," the doctor informed me. I couldn't believe it. It was so sudden. *But he's only 42—he's way too young to be gone…What am I going to do without him? How will I raise my children?* I was in complete shock.

We had just been leaving the hospital after David was being treated for a pulmonary embolism. We were making our way across the parking lot to our van when he couldn't catch his breath and had to be rushed back inside to the emergency room. He died shortly after.

I was escorted to a private consultation room where I was told I could call family members to inform them of David's passing. My mind seemed frozen. I could hardly formulate whom I needed to call let alone their phone numbers.

Some hospital personnel came over to me and asked me if I wanted last rites administered over David, noting that he was listed as Catholic in his medical file. I consented to having a priest from a nearby church being called since our parish was quite a distance away. After he arrived and anointed David, the priest left. As I had nothing more to do, I was told I was free to leave.

"Do you want someone to take you home?" some hospital staff member asked me.

"No, thanks...I can make it on my own," I said. I just wanted time to think and felt uncomfortable inconveniencing them.

As I made my way home, I was devastated. However, I reflected that David could have collapsed in the van or at home, and I was glad that had not happened. Since we were still at the hospital parking lot, David had received medical attention more quickly than if we had been anywhere else, even though they couldn't help him.

When I turned onto my street, I noticed a few people gathered in the yard of my next door neighbor, Patti. I assumed she was sharing with them about David being in the hospital. *How do I tell them that David had passed away? David should still be alive. We were young and had four children.* After pulling into my driveway, I slowly got out of my van and made my way over to them. Patti had been watching my children for me so when I reached the group, she told me that my kids weren't at her house anymore. They had gone over to the house of my out-of-town neighbors to feed their dogs and water their plants.

I then told them that David had died. They all offered their sincere condolences. It was comforting to be around good friends but, while I stood there, a strong urge to go into my house swept over me. I ignored the feeling, but then suddenly the group of neighbors seemed to dissipate quickly. I thought it was odd that everyone left so quickly since we normally talked for a while. There was nothing left for me to do but to go home to my empty house.

Since my kids were still over with my neighbor's dogs, I decided to sit down and try to process what had just happened to my life. I wondered how I was going to tell my children about their father's passing. Before I had time to even think though, I suddenly heard a voice whisper in my ear, "David's coming."

Now, there have been times in my life when I have prayed and wondered if it was the Lord really speaking to me. This time, however, I definitely knew that this voice was not something I had formulated, but something outside of myself. It was very real and clear to me. I later heard that when a person audibly hears a voice from God that they are about to face a series of trying circumstances, and this happened in my case.

Right after the voice spoke, a wind rushed over my shoulder and a hazy, whitish oval materialized to my right. I instinctively comprehended that David was in its midst, but I was puzzled because I sensed another being with him. When I afterward pondered who this other being could have been, I came to the conclusion that it might have been an angel. Luke 16:22 points to the idea that angels guide us after death since it says, "The time came when the beggar died and the angels carried him to Abraham's side."

I didn't give this other presence much thought at the time though and mentally began speaking to David. I relayed to him, "I love you."

He responded back, "I love you."

"You have to help me with these kids," I requested.

He replied, "I will." Then he stated, "You will be with me soon."

Those words immediately startled me. I had just lost my husband, and the thought of my kids not having either parent terrified me. I could not handle that foresight so in my mind, I dismissed the beings. The cloudlike formation hesitated and then gently vanished.

After it disappeared, I mulled over what this presence had said. I decided his disturbing last comment could be interpreted in one of three ways. One possibility was that it might be as 2 Peter 3:8 says: "But do not forget this one thing, dear friends: With the Lord a day is like a thousand years, and a thousand years are like a day." Secondly, maybe the end of the world was approaching, and that was why we would be reunited shortly. Or, lastly, it could be that I would pass away soon, a thought that was quite unnerving!

Rattled and yet blessed by this mysterious event, I remained in the house and waited for my children to return home. It didn't take long until they came through the door. With great pain, I shared with them what had happened. I looked at them all—Anna, the oldest was only twelve, Peter was ten, John was six, and Paul had just turned five the previous week. My heart ached with pain from David's death. We attempted to comfort each other but it was still agonizing.

Family members began to trickle in from out of town for the funeral. David's dad and stepmother, his two brothers and their wives, and his three sisters and their families all came. My mother, sister, and brother came up from Florida. My brother-in-law stayed behind to care for my father who had suffered a stroke several months earlier.

The funeral arrangements seemed to be so well orchestrated, with everyone contributing in their own special way. One of David's brothers and his wife arrived first and helped me navigate all the details of the funeral. David's other brother and wife aided in straightening out my financial details and secured a cemetery plot. My mother and sister helped me select a headstone. Friends brought a variety of dinners for us and even paper products, such as toilet paper and paper plates. Other friends and neighbors volunteered to stay at my house during the funeral to prepare for the funeral luncheon. When it was determined that we still needed another dessert for the meal, someone delivered one within fifteen minutes.

The day when we were to receive visitors at the funeral home was emotional for me. I was driven to the funeral home by one of David's brothers and my sister-in-law. As we pulled into a parking spot in front of the building, I felt so weak. I did not know how I was going to get through the next couple of hours. My brother-in-law, noticing my distress, asked, "Do you want to stay in the car for a little bit?"

"Yes, if you don't mind. I'll be in shortly," I replied. After they departed from the car I was all by myself but found this solitude wasn't helping. *I'm just going to have to force myself to go in there and do this.* I exited the car and made my way in the building and into the room assigned to David. I still was a wreck. Then, peering through all the family members who were gathered, I spotted David in his casket. I thought it would be very painful to see him, but a peace suddenly washed over me. I now knew I would be able to cope with the rest of the day's proceedings, and indeed, I was able to receive all the kind people who came to pay their respects. When the end of the visitation time came though, I was exhausted both mentally and physically.

The next day was the funeral, and we all got ready. Someone drove us to the church and when I first entered it, I began to peer about to see who had come, but quickly found that I had to stop looking. It was so overwhelming to think that all these kind people were thoughtful enough to come to support us and to see their sad faces. I turned my eyes downward and made my way to my seat up front. Father Ed gave a touching tribute and came up and hugged me warmly during the time of greeting. Being surrounded by family and friends gave me the ability to get through the rest of the Mass and burial service.

Most of our family members left the following day except for my mother and sister, who stayed for the next week and helped me transition back into everyday life. It was comforting not having everyone leave at one time, but after they did, I felt like everything was surreal and that I was floating along in a bubble. A knot in my stomach was my constant companion, which made it difficult to eat anything. The only thing I managed to get down was some flavored carbonated water.

I kept mulling over the recent events, and it amazed me how the Lord seemingly had been preparing me for this traumatic event. Two months before David died, as many families do on Memorial Day, we had visited the cemetery to place flowers on David's mother's grave. After doing so, we meandered among the various grave markers, commenting on their inscriptions. "Look at this gravestone. This person was just an infant. . . . Look here; this couple passed away within a week of each other." I discovered one particular stone inscribed with John 3:16. I thought to myself that if ever anyone in my family was buried in this cemetery, I would like to have that verse written on the headstone. That way, anyone passing by might notice that Bible quote being on two headstones and might be motivated to look it up if they were unfamiliar with it or at least be reminded of it. When I was asked by the monument maker what I wanted on David's headstone, I was prepared and thus directed, "John 3:16."

Shortly before David's passing, in my daily routine of reading the Bible, I began to read the first chapter of the book of Job. That day, for some reason, the twenty-first verse seemed to stick out at me with a greater intensity than the rest of the chapter. It said, "Naked I came from my mother's womb, and naked I will depart. The Lord gave and the Lord has taken away; may the name of the Lord be praised." Seemingly, the Holy Spirit was speaking to me through this verse, foreshadowing what was going to occur with David.

Then on the Sunday morning that David was supposed to be released from the hospital, I had gone to church with my children. As Father Ed was delivering his sermon, his voice suddenly seemed to grow louder to me. Then, a voice from nowhere seemed to whisper that the words were for specifically for me. Father Ed proclaimed, "You will have pain in your life, but don't focus on the cross, but on the resurrection." I reflected to myself right there, *"Okay, I'll file that away in my mind until I need it."* Little did I know that I would need those words that very afternoon when David passed away.

After David's death, I attempted to keep things as normal as possible for my children, but I had difficulty focusing on anything. I missed David and wondered about him. Was he in heaven? Could he look down from where he was and see us? Did he see how we were affected from his absence?

In my desire to picture what he might be doing, I scrutinized the Bible for any relevant passages and read a few Christian books about death. I just wanted any insights about life after passing from this earth. Probably due to my Catholic upbringing, I always believed that the spirit of a person remained alive after death and could interact with those still on earth. However, I wanted to find Scripture that backed up this belief. Exodus 3 had a story about God telling Moses that He is the God of Abraham, Isaac, and of Jacob. Referring to them in the present tense, even though they had passed away many years before, indicated their continuing existence. This position was later justified in Matthew 22:31-32 that stated, "But about the resurrection of the dead—have you not read what God said to you, 'I am the God of Abraham, the God of Isaac, and the God of Jacob'? He is not the God of the dead but of the living." Then there were passages in the New Testament gospels where Moses and Elijah appear and converse with Jesus even though they had been dead for years.

I also found two passages in the Bible that seem to indicate that those who have passed on may even be aware of activity on this earth. The first was Hebrews 12:1 that says, "Therefore, since we are surrounded by such a great cloud of witnesses, let us throw off everything that hinders and the sin that so easily entangles." What else would the "cloud of witness" be except for those Christians who have gone on to heaven before us?

The other verse was John 8:56 where Jesus, talking to some Jews, states, "Your father Abraham rejoiced at the thought of seeing my day; he saw it and was glad." Abraham was not living on this earth when Jesus was born or crucified, yet Jesus claims Abraham saw His return. This would mean that Abraham was still aware of events occurring on earth long after he passed away.

Perhaps the most insightful look into life after death appears in Luke 16. It speaks about a wealthy man and a beggar man named Lazarus who both die. Lazarus was escorted to Abraham's side, which I pictured as heaven. The wealthy man descended to hell where he was tormented. The rich man was able to see Lazarus by Abraham's side and requests that Lazarus dip his hand in water and cool his tongue. Abraham responds that there is a great chasm between the two places, which cannot be crossed. The wealthy man then requests that Abraham send Lazarus to his five brothers on earth to warn them of the consequences. Making such a request to Lazarus would signify that the wealthy man is still aware of his brothers who were still living on earth. It additionally hints of the possibility of those in heaven having the capability of returning to the earth in some form or other.

Beyond finding Scripture to support the idea that someone is still aware of earthly matters after death, I experienced another thing that made it seem like David was indeed still present in a spirit form. Immediately after his death, the lamp that hung over our kitchen table began to blink sporadically. I wondered if possibly David was using this lamp to show his presence. It certainly seemed plausible to me, as we had lived in this house for nine years and this light had never acted this way in the past.

Anna also had an experience with the lamp that seemed to also confirm this notion. I was fixing breakfast for Anna in the kitchen before she had to be at school. I then remembered that I had failed to wheel the garbage cans out to the street for pickup that day. I left to tend to this chore and when I returned, Anna claimed that a ball of light from this fixture flashed across the kitchen in my absence. I was amazed at this and continued to believe that the blinking light may have been prompted by my husband.

This kitchen light continued to flicker randomly for months. The last time it flickered was when my son John, then seven, had just been diagnosed with Hodgkin's disease. He and his younger brother, Paul, were upstairs asleep in their bedroom. My two older children, Anna and Peter, were sitting on the couch in the living room when the light began to turn on and off. In my frustration, I turned toward it as if I was addressing David and exclaimed, "Fine, leave me down here with a deathly sick child!" Anna and Peter began laughing that I had berated the kitchen light and rolled about on the couch giggling. It never blinked again.

I also believed David came into my life in other ways. I once had the distinct perception that I had just walked through him while climbing the stairs of our house. However, I usually sensed him at night. It often seemed as though he would come into my bedroom, or at other times, I would have dreams about him.

Since I felt that he "visited" me from time to time, I would talk to him about various things in my life. It was probably blasphemous to do so, yet I was drawn to connecting with him. I shared various issues with him and answers would seemingly become apparent. One such incident occurred when my hot water tank was leaking. I called a plumber to look at it, and he recommended replacing it. It was late in the day, so he said he would return the next morning to install a new one. After he left, I wondered if it was really necessary to replace it, since the leak was small and the heater seemingly was working just fine. In my mind, I asked David about it, and immediately the thought came to put a cap on the spout to solve the problem. I had no idea if it was even a possible solution.

I planned on calling the plumber early in the morning to ask about this possibility, but he arrived at my door before I had a chance to do so. I questioned him about this alternative. He replied that he thought it might work, but wondered if such an item was available and, if they were, if the threads would go the right way. I told him I didn't know, but that I was going to look into finding a cap instead of installing a new hot water tank.

After he left, I drove to the hardware store and described the problem to the clerk at the checkout and inquired about this possible piece. He informed me that indeed such an item existed and they had them in stock. I further pressed if people ever used them for such an application as what I planned. The clerk stated they were used for that purpose all the time. Even though I had no idea about such a cap, somehow the solution was able to come to me and I believe that somehow David influenced it.

David's presence also seemed close to me through the radio. Right after David's death, a song became popular called, "One Sweet Day" sung by Mariah Carey and Boyz II Men. The lyrics spoke of someone passing before their time and the rejoicing that would occur when the separated parties would be reunited someday in heaven. I realize that many people can relate strongly to various songs and feel like it was written just for them. However, because popular songs do not often deal with the death of a loved one and I was sensitive to relate anything to David, I contemplated that maybe this was more than a coincidence. Every time I heard it played, tears would well up in my eyes. It was especially moving as it happened to come on my van radio the night I was pulling out of the garage to take my oldest son, Peter, to his first high school dance. I had been feeling sorrowful that David was not present to witness the event, but that song made me feel that it was almost a sign that David was present. It brought me comfort and pain at the same time.

It soon reached the point where I thought about David all the time, and I knew it might be unhealthy. Finally, one night when I supposed he entered my bedroom, I "told" him that I needed to move on from thinking about him and his presence was preventing that. I felt as though I was being drawn into a world I was not yet part of, and I told him he could not continue to infiltrate my thoughts. I felt that he remained with me until I fell asleep, but the visits did end, either through his lack of returning or my determination to stop seeking him.

I obviously didn't stop thinking of David periodically over the years. It always amazed me what would set me off, like seeing another coffee mug like the one he took to work each day sitting at my hairdresser's station. Another time it was getting a whiff of the cologne that he wore from a man passing by me. Just seeing an article in the local newspaper about the company he worked for threw me back to some of the stories he shared from his workplace. At first it was extremely painful but, as time continued, fewer things became triggers, and when they did appear, they slowly became bitter-sweet memories.

I never heard the "One Sweet Day" song again after the first couple of years. After all, it had come out in 1995 and I rarely listened to the radio. When I did, I usually tuned into a Christian music station. Then one day, as I was rewriting and approving some changes that my son Paul had made to this chapter on David, I heard it again. I had spent the morning concentrating almost solely on this chapter about his passing and decided to take a break and go to the local Y to swim. After completing my usual routine of swimming laps and then packing up to go, this song came on over their speaker system. While I often listened to the music they played over the intercom, they usually played a variety of genres like country, Christian, and pop songs so it wasn't like it was on one of their standard taped background selections. Because I had not heard it for such a long time and I just "happened" to be reflecting on him on that very day, it made me feel that David still was caringly looking over me.

Anna, when she was in her early twenties, also had an especially touching episode as well. She had joined the Peace Corps and was serving in Morocco when she downloaded a group of songs onto her computer. As she sat at her computer working on her assignment of assisting the local artisans to sell their wares, one particular tune caught her attention. The words played, "As long as one and one is two / There could never be a father / Who loved his daughter more than I love you." Other verses spoke of going to the meadow and viewing stars, and fishing, all of which David had done with her when she was young. Furthermore, the father described in the lyrics did not seem to be physically present with the girl in the song.

However, the most telling part of the song included these words: "But you don't need to waste your time / Worryin' about the market place / Try to help the human race / Struggling to survive its harshest night." What might be odd words for anyone else fit perfectly for Anna; she was volunteering to help people (help the human race), especially in the business sector (market place), and she faced harsh conditions of summer heat without air-conditioning and cold winter nights without heat (harshest night). The music had such a mystical and haunting quality, and it all just seemed to fit her situation perfectly.

Anna was moved to look up the name of the song and discovered it was entitled, "Father and Daughter" by Paul Simon, and came from the album named *Surprise*. Because the song correlated so closely to her relationship with her father and the name of the album was so appropriate to what she felt, Anna believed that her father was somehow connecting to her through this song.

Although there is no definitive proof of what happens in the afterlife, I reflected on these scriptural passages and the chance happenings that I have experienced since David passed on from this world. Doing so makes me confident that our spirits continue to exist and love can transcend death.

Lyrics to the song "One Sweet Day"
http://www.metrolyrics.com/one-sweet-day-lyrics-mariah-carey.html

Sorry I've never told you
All I wanted to say
And now it's too late to hold you
'Cause you've flown away
So far away

Never had I imagined
Living without your smile
Feeling and knowing you hear me
It keeps me alive
Alive

[Chorus:]
And I know you're shining down on me from heaven
Like so many friends we've lost along the way
And I know eventually we'll be together
One sweet day
(picture a little scene from heaven)

Darling I never showed you
Assumed you'd always be there (always)
I took your presence for granted
But I always cared (but I always cared)
And I miss the love we shared

[Chorus]

Although the sun will never shine the same again
I'll always look to a brighter day
(yeah) Lord I know when I lay me down to sleep
You will always listen as I pray

[Chorus x2]

Sorry I never told you
All I wanted to say

Lyrics to the song "Father and Daughter"
http://www.paulsimon.com

If you leap awake in the mirror of a bad dream
And for a fraction of a second you can't remember
where you are
Just open your window and follow your memory
upstream
To the meadow in the mountain where we counted
every falling star

I believe a light that shines on you will shine on you
forever
And though I can't guarantee there's nothing scary
hiding under your bed
I'm gonna stand guard like a postcard of a Golden
Retriever
And never leave 'til I leave you with a sweet dream in
your bed

I'm gonna watch you shine
Gonna watch you grow
Gonna paint a sign
So you'll always know
As long as one and one is two
There could never be a father
Who loved his daughter more than I love you

Trust your intuition
It's just like goin' fishin'
You cast your line and hope you get a bite
But you don't need to waste your time
Worryin' about the market place

Try to help the human race
Struggling to survive its harshest night

I'm gonna watch you shine
Gonna watch you grow
Gonna paint a sign
So you'll always know
As long as one and one is two
There could never be a father
Who loved his daughter more than I love you.

Scripture

Mark 12:26-27: "Now about the dead rising—have you not read in the book of Moses, in the account of the bush, how God said to him, 'I am the God of Abraham, the God of Isaac, and the God of Jacob'? He is not the God of the dead, but of the living. You are badly mistaken!"

1 Thessalonians 4:13-14, 16-17:
Brothers, we do want you to be ignorant about those who fall asleep, or to grieve like the rest of men, who have no hope. We believe that Jesus died and rose again and so we believe that God will bring with Jesus those who have fallen asleep in him.

For the Lord himself will come down from heaven, with a loud command, with the voice of the archangel and with the trumpet call of God, and the dead in Christ will rise first. After that, we who are still alive and are left will be caught up together with them in the clouds to meet the Lord in the air. And so we will be with the Lord forever.

Hebrews 12:1: Therefore, since we are surrounded by such a great cloud of witnesses, let us throw off everything that hinders and the sin that so easily entangles, and let us run with perseverance the race marked out for us.

John 8:56: "Your father Abraham rejoiced to see my day: and he saw it, and was glad."

Luke 16:19-31:

"There was a rich man who was dressed in purple and fine linen and lived in luxury every day. At his gate was laid a beggar named Lazarus, covered with sores and longing to eat what fell from the rich man's table. Even the dogs came and licked his sores.

"The time came when the beggar died and the angels carried him to Abraham's side. The rich man also died and was buried. In hell, where he was in torment, he looked up and saw Abraham far away, with Lazarus by his side. So he called to him, 'Father Abraham, have pity on me and send Lazarus to dip the tip of his finger in water and cool my tongue, because I am in agony in this fire.'

"But Abraham replied, 'Son, remember that in your lifetime you received your good things, while Lazarus received bad things, but now he is comforted here and you are in agony. And besides all this, between us and you a great chasm has been fixed, so that those who want to go from here to you cannot, nor can anyone cross over from there to us.'

"He answered, 'Then I beg you, father, send Lazarus to my father's house, for I have five brothers. Let him warn them, so that they will not also come to this place of torment.'

"Abraham replied, 'They have Moses and the Prophets; let them listen to them.'

"'No, father Abraham,' he said, 'but if someone from the dead goes to them, they will repent.'

"He said to him, 'If they do not listen to Moses and the Prophets, they will not be convinced even if someone rises from the dead.'"

—14—

Tithing/Giving to the Lord

"Your checkbook reflects what kind of Christian you are," announced the man on the radio. "To whom are most of your checks written?" I was listening to a Christian station on my way to the grocery store. The speaker added, "When you cheerfully give to others, the Lord will reward you with even more."

The speaker went on to share the story about William Colgate, who first became a partner in a soap company and then the sole owner. Colgate always made sure he faithfully tithed, or gave ten percent of his income. His company grew more and more successful, so he kept increasing his tithe until he was donating half of his earnings. The more Colgate gave the more it seemed that his company was successful and eventually his company became a household name.

The radio program referred to the scriptural basis for this phenomenon where it seems like our giving multiplies in return. They quoted Proverbs 3:9-10 that states that we are to honor God with our firstfruits, and then our barns and vats would overflow with crops and new wine. Translated into more modern terms, when we give first to others, we will not be in want and will experience many blessings. Sometimes it can be in the form of money, but other times it can be by having good things happen in our lives.

In Malachi 3:10, it states that this is one area where we are encouraged to test the Lord. He says when we give that He will "throw open the floodgates of heaven and pour out so much blessing that you will not have room enough for it."

Although the Old Testament referred to the amount to give as a tithe or ten percent of one's resources, the New Testament does not lay down such stipulations. Instead, this principle aligns itself with the major emphasis of the new covenant, which is one of obedience rather than following set rules. In other words, give how much and to whom you believe the Lord is asking you to give.

As I listened to the program, I was shocked. I was unsure if I really wanted to have less money than I could possibly have. Although I knew my father had been a generous giver to the church and others, I did not usually tithe as I was still a new Christian and had not heard much about it. However, that radio show made an impact upon me. It made sense that the amount you give away reflects the degree to which you trust God to provide for you.

I questioned whether I could ask my husband to give, as I was a stay-at-home mother, not officially earning the money. However, I did receive some monetary gifts now and then, such as money given to me on my birthdays. I vowed to begin by giving ten percent from these sources and then gradually encouraged David to participate in this practice also.

About three years after practicing this principle, David and I planned to trade in our Ford Taurus station wagon and purchase a new van. Our vehicle was eight years old, but it had only fifty-six thousand miles on it and it was in rather good shape. However, the car dealership was only going to offer us eight hundred dollars for it even though the Blue Book value was actually closer to three or four thousand dollars. As a result, we were contemplating selling the car ourselves. Then, on the next Sunday as I was sitting in church, an overwhelming feeling suddenly came over me. I felt like we were supposed to give our Taurus to David's youngest sister and her husband, who were in need of a car.

I mentioned to David the possibility of doing this, and he immediately agreed, which surprised me. I thought he might be resistant. I smugly thought in my heart that this would be a good lesson for David to witness how the Lord rewards those who give. I was filled with anticipation for how this would occur.

However, unknown to me at the time, the lesson was meant for me, not David. Not long later, David died. In addition to the pain of losing David, I was unsure how I would fare financially without having David present bringing home an income. I had not worked in twelve years and had four children to support. As the Lord worked it, not only was I able to survive, I was even able to continue my dream of being able to stay at home full time for many years. Logically, this should not have been possible, but the Lord financially provided for us in a variety of ways. I believe was because of my faithfulness in tithing that this occurred.

Over the years, I continued to tithe. I used ten percent as a basis and then gave additionally as I felt the Lord leading. It seemed once I got in the habit of giving, it became less painful than when I first began, as I always seemed to receive more back than what I gave.

Not only did we gain financially, but we also seemed to have a multitude of personal blessings. My children developed positive characters, formed solid friendships, prospered in their schooling, obtained great opportunities and jobs, and found wonderful spouses.

Although I cannot prove a direct correlation between my contributing and positive financial circumstances and blessings in our family, I will continue to participate in this practice!

Scripture

Proverbs 3:9-10: Honor the LORD with your wealth, with the firstfruits of all your crops; then your barns will be filled to overflowing, and your vats will brim over with new wine.

Proverbs 28:27: He who gives to the poor will lack nothing, but he who closes his eyes to them receives many curses.

Malachi 3:9-12: "You are under a curse—the whole nation of you—because you are robbing me. Bring the whole tithe into the storehouse, that there may be food in my house. Test me in this," says the LORD Almighty, "and see if I will not throw open the floodgates of heaven and pour out so much blessing that you will not have room enough for it. I will prevent pests from devouring your crops, and the vines in your fields will not cast their fruit," says the LORD Almighty. "Then all the nations will call you blessed, for yours will be a delightful land," says the LORD Almighty.

Luke 6:38: "Give, and it will be given to you. A good measure, pressed down, shaken together and running over, will be poured into your lap. For with the measure you use, it will be measured to you."

2 Corinthians 9:6: Remember this: Whoever sows sparingly will also reap sparingly, and whoever sows generously will also reap generously.

—15—

Carrying Each Other's Burdens

"How long have you had that lump?" the doctor inquired of John, my seven-year-old son.

"I've always had it," he blankly replied. What was he saying? I had never seen it before, but I suppose a young child was prone to saying such things.

The growth under his arm was almost as large as a golf ball. We had just been to Florida for Easter vacation a couple of weeks earlier to visit my mother, sister, and her husband. While John had often been in a bathing suit, I had not noticed this immense bulge at the time, but it would have been difficult to notice when his arms were down.

The doctor declared, "You need to get this looked at by a surgeon as soon as possible." Because it was a Friday, we had to wait until Monday to see the surgeon, which meant I was on edge all weekend. I knew lumps were trouble, and floating somewhere in the very back of my mind was the word '*cancer*.'

Finally, Monday arrived and the surgeon examined John. He then informed me, "This needs to be biopsied as soon as possible. I'm scheduling surgery for tomorrow, so be back here at six in the morning." Fear began to permeate my body. This was not a good sign.

We went home to get ready to return the following day. I kept trying to convince myself that it was nothing serious. Maybe it was his lymph nodes just responding to the strep he had been recently diagnosed with, which was the original reason I had taken John to see the doctor. However, I needed support from someone to deal with the stress if this lump was going to prove to be something far more serious. Consequently, I decided to call Bob, a divorced man I had become friends with at church, and asked him to pray for the next day's proceedings. When I explained the situation to him, he asked, "Do you want me to come and sit with you at the hospital?"

"No, I don't want you to miss work, but thanks for the offer. I would be great if you could pray for us, though," I responded. I appreciated his gesture, but I did not want this man to sacrifice his time. I kept trying to convince myself that John's condition was not all that serious anyway.

The next morning, we arose at what felt like the middle of the night and arrived at the hospital at our assigned time. John was prepared for surgery and then he was given time to play with some toys until they were ready for him. When the medical staff came to get him, I struggled to maintain composure. My child was being taken away by people he didn't know and was about to undergo surgery. I would not be present to comfort him if he needed me. *He looked so scared!* All I could do was stand there and helplessly watch as they wheeled him away on a gurney. When he was out of sight, I dejectedly retreated to the waiting room.

Once there, I heard a group of people talking as they anxiously awaited word about their child. Dire news might await them, but I was sure I would receive a more upbeat report. I attempted to remain calm as I began to read a book that my friend, Nancy, had given me for my birthday that year. A couple of hours later, a doctor arrived in the waiting room and walked over to me.

"We believe from the initial results that John has Hodgkin's disease," the doctor shared. *What? How could this be?* I was very worried about my son. I had lost David only ten months ago and was just beginning to recover some aspects of normalcy. Now this man was saying my seven-year-old son had cancer. *No, this could not be happening! How could God allow this tragedy so close after David's death?* God was now letting me to face another major trial in my life so shortly after my husband's death. I felt like I was being blindsided.

As I was attempting to digest this news, I was led to a consultation room to discuss the specifics of what would transpire next. The first thing the physician asked was, "Do you work?"

I told him that I didn't and he was glad.

His question made me think back to an odd answer to prayer I had received a few weeks earlier. I had prayed about applying for a part-time family and consumer sciences position that had become available at our local high school. The only answer I thought I heard from God was not to do so because it would be "a stumbling block." I had contemplated the meaning of such an odd answer, but I obeyed and I did not submit my résumé. Now, three weeks later, I understood why I had received that response. This job would have interfered with my ability to help John through the cancer treatments.

My mind returned to the conversation as the doctor attempted to comfort me and claimed, "If someone had to get cancer, this is the one to get. We can nearly use the word *'cure'* in connection this particular cancer." That was encouraging, but his consolations failed to alleviate my torment. All I comprehended was that I had a very sick child with cancer.

Shortly after the doctor said this to me, someone came in and informed me that I could go back and see John in the recovery room.

As I approached his bed, my stomach tightened even more. He looked as though he had been beaten. I am not sure what gave me that impression but it made me feel sick. I sat down in a chair by John's bed, drawing on all my strength to remain upbeat and strong for him. However, I was so distraught that I felt like jumping out the window beside me. It was all so overwhelming. In my mind, I shrieked to the Lord from the depths of my soul, barely able to maintain my sanity.

Just then I looked up and saw Bob, the man I had phoned the night before to pray over this day's proceedings. I felt like he was divinely sent as rays of light seemed to be radiating from behind him as he opened the doors of the recovery room. He had decided to ignore my rebuff and left work early to support me. The Lord was so good. He knew ahead of time that I would not be able to handle the ordeal and laid it upon Bob's heart to be with me. I am eternally grateful that Bob heeded the Lord's prompting as I definitely needed someone with me. There were many times in my life the Lord had planted an idea in my mind to do something for someone and so many times I had ignored doing it. I was grateful Bob had instead listened to the Holy Spirit's prompting and came to the hospital.

Soon, the doctor returned and encouraged me to have John receive his first dose of chemotherapy right then, so I agreed. Bob remained with us until the chemotherapy was completed, and then helped us depart from the hospital with all our belongings. Since it was rather late at night now, I was even more thankful that Bob was there to escort us to our van.

Once arriving at home and not having Bob's comforting presence, I again began to feel defeated. All the pressures of bringing up four children alone, plus now having to deal with one of them fighting cancer, were just too much. I prayed and asked the Lord to sustain me. I felt so fragile, but I made it through the night.

John was now scheduled to receive chemotherapy twice a month for the next four months. Typical treatment for Hodgkin's involved both chemotherapy and radiation. However, this hospital was currently participating in a study to determine if radiation was truly needed in such cases. Some candidates received both chemotherapy and radiation, while others received only chemotherapy. I was asked if I wanted John to participate. I questioned the doctor about the effectiveness of chemotherapy alone, and he assured me the evidence supported its success. I then consented to have John in this study.

Prior to receiving his next dose, John had to undergo surgery to insert a port into one of the veins in his upper chest. This device was a thin, soft catheter tube that would run through this vein all the way to his heart and would help protect the vein during treatment. The other end of this tube would be an entry point for the cancer-fighting medicine and for nurses to draw blood for the many required blood tests.

I had painfully had learned during John's first operation that to get through this, I would need a comforting friend with me while John underwent surgery. Having another person along would give me strength, divert my attention from worrying, and afford me the added benefit of another set of ears to listen to the doctor's instructions. I asked my high school friend, Peggy, to accompany me this time. She agreed and I was much calmer having her by my side.

After the surgery, the doctor instructed, "Now that John has this port, please notify us if he ever gets a fever. If he gets one, he will have to be hospitalized so we can monitor him to make sure that the infection doesn't spread throughout his whole body."

These words unnerved me. If the scenario the doctor described ever happened, I would want to be with John but would have three other children at home who also needed me. Unable to bear the thought of John alone in the hospital, I was determined he would not fall prey to such a situation. Germs, therefore, became the enemy. I basically confined John to home, screened the health status of all visitors, and became a major supporter of hand sanitizer. Thankfully, the Lord answered my prayers. John never contracted a fever until three days after the port was removed.

After the first dose of chemotherapy, the lump under John's arm completely disappeared. I was unsure if that was how the treatment normally unfolded, but the doctor seemed truly amazed. "The treatment is really working!" he joyfully declared. I preferred to think John's excellent progress was due to the outpouring of the prayers of all my Christian friends on John's behalf.

John was so patient during the lengthy four to five hour sessions that were required to receive his chemotherapy. However, during his last treatment, the smell from the medicine started him fussing before it even began. I was so grateful that it was his final session.

John had to wait a month after his last chemotherapy to make sure he still was cancer-free before he could get his port removed. Once again, I sought someone to be by my side and my neighbor, Wendy, obliged. The surgery went off without any complications and I looked forward to getting this all behind us.

However, I still could not relax. Fear now became my constant companion. *Was that a cough I heard from him? Was that a new mass forming?* Any little sickness evoked worried me.

Once, believing that I had discovered a lump on John's chest, I raced to the doctor, only to discover that he had two fused ribs. Surely this raised area had always been visible, but I had never noticed until I started obsessing about his health.

To further complicate matters, John developed an ailment that his primary care doctor could not diagnosis. "Mom, my hand is starting to swell," he announced one day. And his hand continued to puff up over the next two days. The swelling traveled from his lower arm all the way up to his shoulder. Hurriedly, I scheduled an appointment with his doctor.

"He could have been bitten by a spider, but I can't find any evidence of that. I'm not sure what's causing it," his primary care physician confessed. I'll put him on an antibiotic, and we'll see if that helps." The swelling slowly subsided but the ordeal caused much anxiety for me.

I attempted to fight this new traumatizing lifestyle by pretending life was normal. "Let's go to an amusement park," I suggested one day. There was one about an hour and a half from our home and I thought it could help us all escape from the strain we had been experiencing. Peter asked if he could bring a neighborhood friend, so I let him. John claimed he did not want to go, but he often had temperamental outbursts as a side effect of one of the medicines that he was still required to take. I decided to ignore his negative response, reflecting how he had enjoyed this type of activity in the past. The next day, we all piled into the car and drove off to the park.

As soon as we passed through the gates, however, John announced he did not feel well. When I tried to get him to clarify the problem, he shot back that he had told me he did not want to come. I stood there berating myself for not listening to him and contemplated what my next step should be. I had just paid the expensive price for admission, and additionally, so had Peter's friend, who was eager to explore the rides.

I decided to cautiously proceed with our visit, but John persisted in being less than enthusiastic. I asked him if there was anything he wanted to do, and he claimed he wanted to play miniature golf. This was practically the only attraction that carried an additional cost, and I was hesitant to spend more money. However, because John was so miserable, I reluctantly paid the fee. After I saw that John's disposition immediately improved when he played, I was more than happy to pay the additional cost.

Luckily, we all ended up enjoying the rest of our day together.

Gradually, I was able to relax as John continued to be cancer free. However, three years later, I was thrown back into deep concern. John's six month checkup indicated that his white blood cell count had dropped drastically, which was not a good sign. After the following checkup showed no improvement, the doctor was concerned and increased the frequency of our appointments from every six months to every month.

Luckily, no signs of cancer resurfaced, and gradually, the examinations were expanded to every two months, three months, and then four months. We eventually returned to the regular six-month schedule. Finally, in the fall of 2006, his white blood cell count registered as normal, and he was officially declared to be in remission. This visit coincided with his ten year anniversary of his diagnosis of cancer, meaning it was almost double the normal time of other Hodgkin's patients to reach this milestone.

I would never have been able to have survived this time in my life without God's grace and so many people coming along side of me. Scripture declares that God is present during our time of need and I did feel His presence strongly. However, I also believe God lays it on people's hearts to be His hands and feet on this earth. Galatians 6:2 instructs us to, "Carry each other's burdens, and in this way you will fulfill the law of Christ."

Being there for others usually involves sacrifice. It can cause an interruption in our schedules, take energy, and can be expensive. I was so blessed to have so many people in my life who were willing to forego their own desires and be there for me. Bob certainly was there as a rock for me as I attempted to parent my children and deal with a seriously ill child. Peggy and Wendy stood by me when John had to have his surgeries. Patti and Jo helped me tremendously at home. Mary, Jeanne, and Ruth, among countless others, fervently prayed for us, which I'm sure helped to produce such a positive outcome for John. All their actions truly showed me God's love for me.

Scripture

Ecclesiastes 4:9-12: Two are better than one, because they have a good return for their work: If one falls down, his friend can help him up. But pity the man who falls and has no one to help him up! Also, if two lie down together, they will keep warm. But how can one keep warm alone? Though one may be overpowered, two can defend themselves. A cord of three strands is not quickly broken.

Proverbs 27:10: Do not forsake your friend and the friend of your father, and do not go to your brother's house when disaster strikes you—better a neighbor nearby than a brother far away.

Galatians 6:2: Carry each other's burdens, and in this way you will fulfill the law of Christ.

16

God Gives Us Freedom
of Choice

Richard, my brother, struggled with the ability to sleep. He didn't know why he had trouble staying asleep for an entire night. He attempted to cut out caffeine, tried various diets, took up running, and looked to meditation. Nothing seemed to work.

Finally, after twenty years of battling this condition, he arrived at the point where he no longer had the energy to get up and go to work. He was forced to quit his job, which devastated him. His wife, Cara, pleaded with him to consult a psychiatrist. Having no other option to alleviate this issue up to this point, he reluctantly agreed to do so. The doctor diagnosed him with depression and prescribed him medication. Relief, however, was not immediately forthcoming. Time was needed to experiment with various drugs and dosages to fit Richard's individual chemistry. In the meantime, Richard spent most of his time curled on the couch.

Cara, his wife, grew more and more concerned that Richard was becoming suicidal and increased her vigilance over him. She rarely left the house but, then one night, she wanted to attend her grandson's birthday party. She was reluctant to leave Richard alone, but he assured her that he would be fine, so she went.

Upon returning home, Cara thought it odd that none of the lights were on in the house, since it was now dark. She entered the house and soon discovered that Richard had taken his life.

Cara notified my family. My mother especially was devastated and felt guilty, wondering if there was a way that she could have prevented it. My sister, also distraught, began to read books about suicides in an attempt to comprehend how he could have done this. She discovered that suicides sometimes can be linked to a genetic predisposition, since this act often times runs in families. This held true in our family, as two of my mother's siblings had previously taken their lives. Somehow that knowledge helped us to cope with what happened.

Beyond the hurt of losing my brother, I also had to deal with another aspect of my brother's passing in such a manner. I contemplated about how the Catholic Church historically supported that anyone who committed suicide was immediately doomed to hell. Thinking that Richard was condemned to torture for eternity was understandably not a pleasant thought for me.

Several years after Richard's death, however, I came across Luke 12:10 that states, "And everyone who speaks a word against the Son of Man will be forgiven, but anyone who blasphemes against the Holy Spirit will not be forgiven." The idea came to my mind that a person would only be condemned to God's absence if he or she failed to acknowledge the Holy Spirit and abide by Him. All other sins that a person could commit—even suicide—would be forgivable. This gave me much comfort believing that this act alone would not determine Richard's ultimate destiny.

I then wondered if he ever had accepted Jesus as his Savior. Although all of us children had grown up in the Catholic Church, we all eventually abandoned that faith. At that time in this church's history, the power of the Holy Spirit was not drawn upon very much. As a result, it had very little impact to make us to appreciate our Lord and want to draw close to Him. Even so, Richard was a very spiritual person. Yet, I have no way of knowing what Richard eventually determined in his heart, as that is a personal matter between God and each person.

God will never force a person to believe in Him, but allows everyone the freedom to choose whether to dedicate their lives to Him or not. I believe all men are exposed to the existence of God as the Bible claims in Romans 1:20, "For since the creation of the world God's invisible qualities—his eternal power and divine nature—have been clearly seen, being understood from what has been made, so that people are without excuse." This means that all men can see evidence of God's existence by observing the world around them. However, although a person can believe in God, that alone will not allow them to spend eternity with God. If you think about it, even Satan, who has no hope of salvation, believes in God. Instead, we must acknowledge our inherent weaknesses and the saving grace of Jesus Christ, and then vow to make Him our Lord of our life. Only then we are assured of being with God after we pass from this world.

However, a person can choose to worship themselves and do whatever pleases them. Since mankind's natural inclination is to do that which goes against God's ways, they will begin to distance themselves from Him. When one continually disobeys what God wants them to do, Romans 1:21 says that we darken our hearts. It says, "For although they knew God, they neither glorified him as God nor gave thanks to him, but their thinking became futile and their foolish hearts were darkened." Ephesians 4:18 and Hebrews 3:12-13 refers to this as a hardening of the heart.

Yet, God never gives up on a person and always desires that they come back into fellowship with Him. In Revelation 3:20, Jesus says, "Here I am! I stand at the door and knock. If anyone hears my voice and opens the door, I will come in and eat with him, and he with me." We first have to choose to open the door though.

I prayed that Richard had answered that bidding and one incident points to the possibility that he had. Cara disclosed to me how once in their marriage she had asked permission to hang a picture of Jesus in their home. Richard had refused. Sometime later, Richard asked Cara as to the whereabouts of the picture. When she informed him of its location, he asked her to retrieve it. He then hung it up in the bedroom that he used for meditation. This report helped to comfort me and I hope that someday we will be reunited in heaven.

Scripture

Luke 12:10: And everyone who speaks a word against the Son of Man will be forgiven, but anyone who blasphemes against the Holy Spirit will not be forgiven.

Ezekiel 18:23: Do I take any pleasure in the death of the wicked? declares the Sovereign LORD. Rather, am I not pleased when they turn from their ways and live?

2 Peter 3:9: The Lord is not slow in keeping his promise, as some understand slowness. He is patient with you, not wanting anyone to perish, but everyone to come to repentance.

Revelation 3:20: Here I am! I stand at the door and knock. If anyone hears my voice and opens the door, I will come in and eat with him, and he with me.

John 12:37-40: Even after Jesus had done all these miraculous signs in their presence, they still would not believe in him. This was to fulfill the word of Isaiah the prophet: "Lord, who has believed our message and to whom has the arm of the Lord been revealed?" For this reason they could not believe, because, as Isaiah says elsewhere: "He has blinded their eyes and deadened their hearts, so they can neither see with their eyes, nor understand with their hearts, nor turn—and I would heal them."

Ephesians 4:18-19: They are darkened in their understanding and separated from the life of God because of the ignorance that is in them due to the hardening of their hearts. Having lost all sensitivity, they have given themselves over to sensuality so as to indulge in every kind of impurity, and they are full of greed.

Hebrews 3:12-13: See to it, brothers, that none of you has a sinful, unbelieving heart that turns away from the living God. But encourage one another daily, as long as it is called "Today," so that none of you may be hardened by sin's deceitfulness.

Romans 1:18-25:

The wrath of God is being revealed from heaven against all the godlessness and wickedness of men, who suppress the truth by their wickedness, since what may be known about God is plain to them, because God has made it plain to them. For since the creation of the world God's invisible qualities—his eternal power and divine nature—have been clearly seen, being understood from what has been made, so that people are without excuse.

For although they knew God, they neither glorified him as God nor gave thanks to him, but their thinking became futile and their foolish hearts were darkened. Although they claimed to be wise, they became fools and exchanged the glory of the immortal God for images made to look like a mortal human being and birds and animals and reptiles. Therefore God gave them over in the sinful desires of their hearts to sexual impurity for the degrading of their bodies with one another. They exchanged the truth about God for a lie, and worshiped and served created things rather than the Creator—who is forever praised. Amen.

17

Trials in Our Life

Thanksgiving was the next day, and excitement filled the air. This year was going to be even more enjoyable than usual. Anna had been away for her first year of college and had been telling me for weeks how much she was looking forward to my home cooking. Her flight had arrived hours ago, but she had dashed off to meet up with her boyfriend from high school. My oldest son, Peter, was a junior in high school. He had been driven to school by his friend, Dave, who would be dropping him off soon. My youngest two children, John and Paul, would be coming through the door about an hour later after riding home on the bus. In the meantime, I decided to begin cooking some of the dishes that I would be serving for the next day. I gathered together the ingredients for making pumpkin pie when the phone rang.

"Mary, this is Dave's dad. The boys have been in an accident. Peter's pretty banged up. He's been life-flighted to Mercy hospital."

My heart sunk.

I was very worried about Peter, but since he didn't say anything about Dave, I worrisomely asked, "How is Dave?"

"Oh, he's okay," Dave's dad assured me. "He was examined at St. Felix's Hospital and has been released."

I was frantically attempting to process what Dave's father was saying. Dave had only been taken to our local hospital while Peter was taken to a large, downtown hospital. There seemed to be a huge difference in care being taken to each of the boys. *Peter must be a bit more than "banged up."*

"Do you know how to get to the hospital?" Dave's father continued.

"I don't know," I replied. My mind was in a fog. All I could think about was that Peter was hurt. My younger son, John, had received his chemotherapy treatments at a nearby hospital, so I thought I should know the way, but I didn't trust myself to be able to find it.

"I'll come over to get you then," Dave's father offered.

"Oh, ok, thanks," I replied, barely knowing what was going on.

I hung up the phone and was immediately flooded with worry, pain, and grief. *My Peter has been in an accident...He probably is in a great deal of pain. I cannot deal with this—I need support!* I telephoned my next-door neighbor, Patti, and relayed to her what had happened. After hearing my desperation, she hung up and immediately came over. When I saw her, I dropped to my knees in front of her. "Why is the Lord allowing me to face another trial? Haven't I had enough to deal with?" I pleaded. Patti told me she didn't know, but she was very compassionate about the situation.

Later, I came to understand from the Scripture that trials are to be expected in this life, but I was beginning to feel like the Biblical character, Job. He faced a multitude of difficulties within a short time of each other. First, raiders took his oxen, donkeys, and camels and put his servants to the sword. Then, fire fell from the sky and burned up his sheep and the rest of his servants. Even his sons and daughters were not spared, as a mighty wind collapsed on them the house where they were feasting. Finally, Job himself was afflicted with "painful sores from the soles of his feet to the top of his head."

Acts 14:22, 1 Peter 4:12, and 1 Thessalonians 3:2-4 all disclose that as Christians, we are to expect struggles in our life. Hebrews 12:7-11 compares how God allows difficulties in our lives to how earthly parents discipline their children to shape their behavior. Although painful at the time and often misunderstood for having to endure it, the person has his or her character developed by going through tough times.

Trails in life seem to attack us not in a singular fashion but one right after the other. If one just occurred, we might be able to muster up the ability to deal with it. However, when faced with many, our fragility comes to the surface more readily.

Often people will point to the comment that God will not give you more than you can handle. I believe this idea originates from 1 Corinthians 10:13b that states, "God is faithful; he will not let you be tempted beyond what you can bear." However, this verse is not referring to trials but to temptation. Instead, I believe that God allows trials to bombard us to the point where we are overwhelmed. Facing serious illnesses, relational issues, and financial woes can force us to turn to God in humility as He is the only source of power we have left to combat these issues. By emptying ourselves and depending solely upon God, we allow God to fully unleash His power in our life. Paul sums up this precept in 2 Corinthians 12:10 when he says he delighted, "in weaknesses, in insults, in hardships, in persecutions, in difficulties. For when I am weak, then I am strong."

Understanding our limits gives us a much greater appreciation of our Lord. Although God may have been previously present in our lives, a greater commitment and willingness to be obedient arises after facing trials. Thus, our relationship with our Creator is developed further.

Without trials in life, one tends to be complacent and prideful. One may attribute their successes to their own abilities and strength because they alone believe they have been responsible for their comfortable position. People who have comfortable lives also are likely to have less compassion for others who face struggles.

However, not all will turn to the Lord in troubling times. A person may have a strong sense of entitlement that life should be pleasant. Then, when hardships arise, anger, bitterness, and resentment may fill their minds as they focus only upon themselves and the pain they are suffering. They question why they have to endure such misfortune and about what type of God would allow this to happen. Some may even abandon their faith completely.

Thus facing trials can act as a test. Does the person seek God or turn away from Him? Additionally, when faced with hard times, do they mainly seek comfort from the Lord or from outside sources or outlets?

There may be occasions when God appears to be absent during a difficult time, which also tests a follower. Will they still adhere to the promises of God, even though they don't feel his presence?

God proclaims that He will never leave or forsake us and may actually be the closest to us as we undergo difficult situations. John 15:1-4 likens God as a gardener and believers as a vine. In caring for vegetation, a plant flourishes more when superfluous or undesirable twigs, branches, or roots are trimmed. Likening this to human condition, as one experiences loss through the Lord, they will eventually benefit, even though the event or events are painful at the moment. It is also comforting to consider that the vine dresser is never nearer to the plant than when he is trimming it. This can be translated into our Lord being the closest to us during trying situations.

Although trials are inevitable in a Christian's life, we are told they will be only for a time. Job, with all his rash of difficulties eventually reached a place of peace. In fact, Job 42:12 reveals that Job's life after enduring the trials was blessed more than his life before the trials.

However, I was not yet fully aware of the positive function of the difficulties in life when I heard that son Peter had been hurt in an accident. I was still in the midst of dealing with the grief at this point.

A few minutes after Patti arrived, Anna walked through the door. A flood of relief poured over me. Being the oldest child, I had come to depend upon her for support and comfort. I confided in her frequently and often asked her advice about issues. She would be concerned about Peter about as much as me. With her by my side, I could attempt driving to the hospital. When Dave's dad arrived shortly afterwards, I informed him that he no longer needed to drive me, since I was confident Anna and I could make it together.

After arriving at the hospital and walking through the doors of the emergency room, I noticed that Dave and his mother were already there. I acknowledged them and then walked up to the admitting desk to ask about Peter. The lady managing the desk stated that Peter was being attended to and instructed me to take a seat, and that she would call me when I could go back to see him. My mind raced as I was left to just speculate about his condition. My face must have revealed my concern because the nurse attempted to reassure me that Peter was going to be fine. Her words failed to give me much comfort though—I needed to see him for myself. Frustrated, I retreated back to where Dave and his parents were, as his dad had arrived while I had been talking to the nurse.

I knew Dave's family well. Since Dave lived just a few streets from us, Peter had been friends with him since elementary school. Dave often was at our house playing ping pong or video games. I had even become acquainted with Carol, his mom, because she was a fellow member of the school PTA.

When Peter and Dave reached their junior year in high school, the two boys wanted to drive to school each day. Although I was initially hesitant, I finally relented and allowed Peter to take his car because a lot of students started driving to school at this age. The regular school buses were overcrowded, and it took twice the time to get to school by bus than by car. They decided that they would take turns as to who would drive each day, and it was Dave who drove that day.

As Anna and I sat down to wait, Dave conveyed what had occurred. After the school day ended, Peter and Dave got into Dave's car. They decided to drive home on a back way, which included a twisting, two-lane road through a rural neighborhood.

The boys busily chatted about what they would do during their upcoming days off. In his excitement, Dave picked up speed. Upon cresting a hill and getting to a winding section of road, Dave pressed the accelerator to go even faster. Merrily, they flew down the road at speeds around 70 miles per hour that had a posted speed limit of 35 miles an hour.

Dave began having a difficult time controlling the car, and it slipped onto the side of the road where an additional strip of pavement had been added. As he attempted to bring the car back onto the main part of the asphalt, he turned the steering wheel in the opposite direction. The vehicle immediately shot uncontrollably across the road and hit a telephone pole on the side of the car where Peter was sitting. The car continued down a steep embankment flanking the road. Finally, the car came to a halt at the bottom of the hill.Dave glanced over at Peter. His head was down, his eyes were closed, and blood was streaming from his mouth. Dave anxiously wondered if he had killed one of his best friends.

Someone in a nearby house heard the crash and called the police, who then notified Dave's dad. An officer arrived quickly, along with an EMS unit, and determined that Peter needed to be rushed to a hospital with a skilled trauma unit. They called to have him life-flighted to a large hospital downtown.

I felt sick as I listened to these details, which made the wait even more unbearable. *Just how bad were Peter's injuries?* Time seemed to crawl, but finally a nurse informed Anna and me that we could go back to see him. We got up and went to a back hallway, where he was lying on a gurney awaiting surgery. It was heart wrenching to see him in such a state. He was thrashing about and groaning, seemingly in immense pain. The nurse informed us that Peter had broken his femur, pelvis, and jaw bones along with bruising his lung where the seatbelt had crossed his chest.

"Peter, how are you?" I tried to say calmingly.

"Ugh, my leg. It's killing me," he moaned as he grabbed it. Up to this point, I had always dreaded having any of my children face surgery. Now all I wanted was to have Peter operated on as quickly as possible so he could be relieved of his misery. Fortunately, it was not long before they came to take him to surgery.

As nighttime approached, I sent Anna home to stay with my younger boys. Dave's mom remained with me, and we went to find a more private waiting room where we could settle in for a while. After finding a quiet alcove, I had nothing to do but to ponder about this situation over and over again. Then, in my misery, I looked up to see my friends Mary and Jeanne enter the room with their husbands. My fellow Christian prayer warriors from my Moms in Touch group were there with me once again to support me. What a blessing they were! Not only did they petition the Lord about the entire surgical procedure, but they helped distract me from the overwhelming distress that threatened to wash over me whenever I reflected upon Peter's condition.

After some time, the doctor arrived to inform us about the surgery. "The operation was successful. The femur was completely broken so we inserted a titanium rod into the middle of the bone for support. He is resting peacefully now and is scheduled to have surgery on his jaw tomorrow." This report gave me much relief. I was thankful to God for answering the prayers, but I was still aware that Peter had a long path to recovery.

My friends left soon after the doctor's report, so Dave's mom and I searched the hospital for a place to get some rest for the night. We found some reclining chairs in a corner of a room and settled in them, but I spent most of the night tossing and turning.

The next day, the surgeon scheduled to operate on Peter's jaw tried to familiarize me with what would happen during the upcoming surgery. "Peter's jaw is broken in several places. After we get in there, we'll determine if he needs to have his jaw wired shut. We'll also be able to tell how many teeth he has lost, since he has some rather big gaps. The procedure should take about three hours. When we're done, I'll come back and let you know how it went." After he departed, I prayed that the Lord would guide his hands and that the operation would go well.

Patti once again supported me by coming to the hospital and waiting with me. Her presence made a stressful situation much more bearable. She helped distract my mind because I helped her cut out paper figures for the preschool class she taught.

After two hours, the doctor excitedly appeared in the waiting room. He exclaimed that the operation had gone extremely well and that wiring Peter's jaw together was unnecessary. He explained how they had used three metal plates to bring the broken jaw pieces back into place. Once this was accomplished, they discovered that Peter's large gaps between his teeth were only a result of his broken jaw and that he had not actually lost any teeth.

I was happy Peter had gotten these two major operations performed, but now Thanksgiving vacation was in full swing and the medical staff was extremely limited. This was unfortunate for Peter since he needed to be tested to see if he had any nerve damage. Since there weren't any personnel available to perform the test, he was placed in a neck brace as a precaution. He additionally was restricted from having any food or drinks and put on an IV. The only thing he could take in was whatever few drops of water he could extract from a small sponge.

Peter was most unhappy at this point. He was trying to recover from two surgeries and could not drink or eat anything. He wanted to communicate with us, too, but the full-head bandage and the neck brace made talking nearly impossible. Also, the multitude of tubes that were connected to him interfered with his ability to write. He attempted to scribble on paper, but most everything he wrote was illegible.

When Monday morning arrived, Peter was finally evaluated. Thankfully, no nerve damage was determined to have occurred. The neck brace and tubes were removed, and he was finally allowed to begin to drink something and eat soft foods. We were all relieved as none of his injuries had resulted in any permanent disabilities.

Even though there were drawbacks to the accident occurring over the Thanksgiving holiday, it was fortunate in some ways. Anna was already home and did not have to interrupt her studies or find a way home. She was immediately available to visit with him and offer him and me comfort. It helped me having her home because she could watch John and Paul, which allowed me to stay at the hospital with Peter. Her time off extended through Peter's entire hospital stay, except for the last night. On that night, my neighbor Patti and her husband graciously volunteered to come down and stay, so I went home to be with the two younger boys.

After spending eight days in the hospital, Peter was transferred to a rehabilitation facility. During his time there, he received a wheelchair, practiced using crutches, and learned exercises to strengthen his damaged and bed-weary muscles. The staff also taught him specific skills, such as dressing himself, which would enable him to take care of himself in his injured state.

Because Peter had undergone surgery and couldn't move around easily, Peter was at risk for blood clotting, which was especially serious since his father had passed away from a clot. The doctors prescribed Lovenox to be administered twice a day by injection into his side for the next two months. After Peter was discharged, I was designated to perform this unpleasant task. I dreaded this duty so much that Peter claimed I must surely be the first person to experience more pain in giving a shot than the one receiving it.

A variety of support personnel soon visited our home frequently. A physical therapist came twice a week to exercise Peter's muscles, and our school district sent a tutor who came once a week. Since Peter had been enrolled in advanced classes, the tutor was not proficient enough to teach him the lessons. Consequently, Peter basically had to instruct himself. He felt he was falling behind in his classes and missed his friends so, after Christmas vacation, Peter insisted upon returning to school. Since he was confined to a wheelchair, the bus was not an option, which meant I had to drive him. It was a 40-minute trip twice a day and I found myself wishing I didn't have to do it. Then, within a week, a long-term substitute teaching position in my field opened up in the school building adjacent to Peter's. It seemed like the perfect God-given opportunity for me. I inquired about it and obtained the job, so driving up was no longer a problem since I had to teach at the school anyways.

Peter's recovery progressed quickly. When Peter went for his initial checkup with the orthopedic doctor, the doctor handed him a sheet outlining the usual protocol for someone with a broken femur. According to this paper, a person with a broken femur should begin weaning himself from walking aids and be free of them in three months. However, Peter progressed from a wheelchair to crutches and to independently walking in only two months. I believe prayer aided in his speedy recovery.

Peter continued to heal rapidly, and by a year later, he was almost fully recovered. I was so happy how well he had recuperated. However, lumps soon began to appear on Peter's gums. We returned to the doctor, who theorized that Peter's body chemistry was reacting to the plates that had been placed in his jaw. He suggested that Peter have them removed.

Surgery was scheduled, and during the operation, the doctor encountered difficulty in extracting all the plates. A fair amount of time had passed since the original surgery, and calcium deposits now firmly covered them. The surgeon removed two of the plates, but was forced to leave the last one in Peter's jaw. He assured me that Peter would probably be fine but, after some time, another bump developed over the remaining plate. Surgery was once again prescribed and this time the plate was successfully removed with no more growths developing later.

Two years after the horrible car accident, Peter was fully-recovered and could do all the activities he previously enjoyed. This trial had been arduous, especially in light of all the other challenges I had been faced with, but the Lord was with me every step of the way. It also continued to help transform me from relying upon my own strength to looking to God and depending upon His supreme power to live out my life instead.

Scripture

Job 1:8-12: Then the LORD said to Satan, "Have you considered my servant Job? There is no one on earth like him; he is blameless and upright, a man who fears God and shuns evil."

"Does Job fear God for nothing?" Satan replied. "Have you not put a hedge around him and his household and everything he has? You have blessed the work of his hands, so that his flocks and herds are spread throughout the land. But now stretch out your hand and strike everything he has, and he will surely curse you to your face."

The LORD said to Satan, "Very well, then, everything he has is in your hands, but on the man himself do not lay a finger."

Psalm 119:71: It was good for me to be afflicted so that I might learn your decrees.

Acts 14:22b: "We must go through many hardships to enter the kingdom of God," they said.

2 Corinthians 1:8-11:

We do not want you to be uninformed, brothers, about the hardships we suffered in the province of Asia. We were under great pressure, far beyond our ability to endure, so that we despaired even of life. Indeed, in our hearts we felt the sentence of death. But this happened that we might not rely on ourselves but on God, who raises the dead. He has delivered us from such a deadly peril, and he will deliver us. On him we have set our hope that he will continue to deliver us, as you help us by your prayers. Then many will give thanks on our behalf for the gracious favor granted us in answer to the prayers of many.

2 Corinthians 12:10: That is why, for Christ's sake, I delight in weaknesses, in insults, in hardships, in persecutions, in difficulties. For when I am weak, then I am strong.

1 Thessalonians 3:2-4: We sent Timothy, who is our brother and God's fellow worker in spreading the gospel of Christ, to strengthen and encourage you in your faith, so that no one would be unsettled by these trials. You know quite well that we were destined for them. In fact, when we were with you, we kept telling you that we would be persecuted. And it turned out that way, as you well know.

Hebrews 12:7-11:

Endure hardship as discipline; God is treating you as sons. For what son is not disciplined by his father? If you are not disciplined (and everyone undergoes discipline), then you are illegitimate children and not true sons. Moreover, we have all had human fathers who disciplined us and we respected them for it. How much more should we submit to the Father of our spirits and live! Our fathers disciplined us for a little while as they thought best; but God disciplines us for our good, that we may share in his holiness. No discipline seems pleasant at the time, but painful. Later on, however, it produces a harvest of righteousness and peace for those who have been trained by it.

James 1:2-4: Consider it pure joy, my brothers, whenever you face trials of many kinds, because you know that the testing of your faith develops perseverance. Perseverance must finish its work so that you may be mature and complete, not lacking anything.

1 Peter 4:12: Dear friends, do not be surprised at the painful trial you are suffering, as though something strange were happening to you.

John 15:1-4: "I am the true vine, and my Father is the gardener. He cuts off every branch in me that bears no fruit, while every branch that does bear fruit he prunes so that it will be even more fruitful. You are already clean because of the word I have spoken to you. Remain in me, and I will remain in you. No branch can bear fruit by itself; it must remain in the vine. Neither can you bear fruit unless you remain in me."

Job 42:12a: The LORD blessed the latter part of Job's life more than the first.

—18—

Being Anointed
When Facing Sickness

At this time in my life, regular visits to doctors and any tests that they prescribed had become great sources of anxiety. I was certain I would be given some dire news, since so many health issues had arisen in my family in the recent past. Yet, I dutifully continued to get regular checkups.

One such time, I went to get the recommended annual mammogram to catch any early signs of cancer. As I waited for the nurse to return, I pleaded with the Lord for no disease to be present. When the nurse entered the room, she said the doctor was requesting more X-rays on my right breast. I had previously had to do this one other time and it wasn't cancerous, so I tried to calm myself with that thought. However, after she left to take the additional scans to the doctor, my anxiety level began to climb.

When she returned to my room, she asked me to follow her. Fear gripped me. I felt that the physician must have seen something because, otherwise, the technician would have told me that I was free to go.

She escorted me to a small, darkened room where the doctor was sitting in front of an illuminated board that had the films hanging down from the top. He greeted me and pointed to a section on the x-ray and said, "See this spot here? This is a calcium deposit in your breast. Some are cancerous, but not always. Usually we can just aspirate a sample with a needle to determine if the they are cancerous. However, because of the location in your breast, we are going to have to operate."

I could hardly process what he was saying. I felt like our family had more than enough to deal with, and now my children's only surviving parent might have cancer! I didn't want to upset my kids, especially if it wasn't cancer, so I decided to not tell them about the uncertain results. I quietly would undergo the required preoperative tests, blood work, and surgery. If the results proved positive, I would proceed from that point.

Even though my children and I had faced many trials, at least I had always been there to support them through each ordeal. Now, if I had cancer, I fretted that I might not be around to help them, which was very distressing to me. I couldn't picture handing over my children over to anyone if anything happened to me.

I decided to make an appointment to see Father Ken, who had formerly been the pastor at St. Steven's, but was now serving in another nearby parish. I believed him to be a man very close to the Lord who could plead my case before God. When I shared my fears with him, he prayed over me and anointed me with oil. This followed the scriptural instructions given in James 5:14-15 that says, "Is anyone among you sick? Let them call the elders of the church to pray over them and anoint them with oil in the name of the Lord. And the prayer offered in faith will make the sick person well; the Lord will raise them up. If they have sinned, they will be forgiven." I left feeling much peace and comfort.

On the day of the surgery, I asked one of my neighbors, Jo, if she would drive me to the hospital. She kindly agreed and even remained at the hospital during the procedure, which was a blessing to me.

After the operation, I was told that everything went well, but I wouldn't know the results until a few days later. Jo then drove me home, situated me in bed, filled my prescriptions, and brought over some food for my family for dinner. Additionally, she continued to keep tabs on me during the first twenty-four hours after my surgery, since the hospital had pressed for someone to do this. She did all this all the while joining me in keeping the day's event a secret from my children. She truly exhibited Christ's sacrificial love for me.

Thankfully, I received a call from the doctor a few days later that the calcium deposits were not cancerous and that I was going to be fine. I was very relieved and thanked God for being merciful. Reflecting back on the experience, I often wondered if I would have fared as well if I had not sought out Father Ken and received his prayers and been anointed with oil. In any event, I was glad I did.

Scripture

James 5:14-15: Is any one of you sick? He should call the elders of the church to pray over him and anoint him with oil in the name of the Lord. And the prayer offered in faith will make the sick person well; the Lord will raise him up. If he has sinned, he will be forgiven.

—19—

Dealing With Worry and Stress

" *Is my van spinning on ice? What's going on? Am I having a stroke?"* I wondered. I felt like something had snapped in my head and it seemed as though the world was swirling about me. It scared me. I didn't understand what was happening and could barely see, especially through the nighttime darkness. *"Try to stay in your lane so you don't hit another car,"* I thought to myself. Although difficult, I pressed on the brake and gradually slowed down as I approached the small hill at the entrance of my street.

Thankfully no cars were around, so I sat at the stop sign for a moment and tried to calm down a bit. Normalcy was beginning to return, but my heart was pounding furiously. I'm not far from home. I can make it, I convinced myself. I eventually started up again and negotiated the left-hand turn leading to my house. I surmised that it might be better to stop first at Wendy's house before going home to care for my kids. Wendy was a good friend of mine who lived just across the street from me.

If I stopped at her house first, I could regain my composure before facing my boys, whom I had left at home while I took Anna to her ballet class.

Wendy ended up taking me to the hospital to make sure nothing serious had occurred. The medical staff ran some tests, but nothing out of the ordinary was found. They kept me overnight as a precaution but, as nothing surfaced, they released the next morning. Thankfully, that episode never repeated itself.

It concerned me that with all the trials I was facing, that my stress was beginning to manifest itself physically in my body. In eight years' time, both my husband and my father had passed away and my brother committed suicide. I had one son diagnosed with cancer and another one involved in a nasty car accident, all along with all the other normal problems that everyone faces.

I longed to have a break from life's trials, but they continually seemed to be coming one right after another. I was always on edge, always expecting more to befall me at any moment. Discouragement and anxiety began to permeate my life.

I knew in my heart that a child of God should not be feeling such despondency because He did not create us to live in such a manner. Galatians 5:22 shares what qualities we should possess as an outcome of having the Spirit in our life. One of them is joy, which I was not experiencing.

It is a misconception that joy is happiness. Happiness is dependent upon circumstances, and those had been difficult in recent years. Joy comes from realizing that God is in control and ultimately fashions events to glorify Himself and that this world is not the end of the story.

Recently, I was concentrating upon all the difficult things that were happening horizontally around me, instead of looking vertically up to God. I considered that if I focused more upon God in my life, the things that were bringing me down would have less of a chance to infiltrate my mind.

To combat this negativity that entered my life, I reflected that our thoughts have a powerful influence upon our lives. No action in our life occurs without us first contemplating about it—either positively or negatively. The same holds true about our mental disposition. If we allow our mind to focus only on the negative things, we will be pessimistic. If we establish our minds on positive things, we will be cheerful.

Scripture encourages us to control what we allow ourselves to dwell on. Philippians 4:8 admonishes us to concentrate on those things that are true, noble, right, pure, lovely, admirable, excellent, or praiseworthy. If we adhere to that precept, those traits should manifest themselves in us.

I also reflected upon the passage in the first chapter of Job where God and Satan are having a conversation. It says, "Then the LORD said to Satan, "Have you considered my servant Job? There is no one on earth like him; he is blameless and upright, a man who fears God and shuns evil." "Does Job fear God for nothing?" Satan replied. "Have you not put a hedge around him and his household and everything he has? You have blessed the work of his hands, so that his flocks and herds are spread throughout the land. But now stretch out your hand and strike everything he has, and he will surely curse you to your face." The LORD said to Satan, "Very well, then, everything he has is in your power, but on the man himself do not lay a finger." To me, this passage exposed the fact that God is well aware of our struggles and even allows them. Somehow it brought me comfort to know any difficulty that I faced had first passed through God's loving hands, and He had allowed it for whatever reason. Nothing that I could have done could have prevented these mishaps from occurring. This knowledge allowed me to be released from feeling guilty about my trials.

Of course, there are trials that are the result of our own misbehavior. Yet, God is a God of new beginnings and He can eventually bring good out of bad when we turn to Him.

Armed with these particular ideas, I vowed to center my thoughts on God and His love for me to fight against my feelings of despair. In addition to reading my Bible and praying, I determined to immerse myself in Christian praise music and purchased some worship CDs. I played them as I did tasks around the house and in the car. This helped to shift my thoughts to God and things of heaven and away from the issues I had on this earth. This strategy seemed to work as gradually my disposition improved and I eventually experienced joy and, later, happiness in my life.

Our minds are powerful and what we choose to think about will shape us. Since trials are to be expected in this life, they can easily overtake us as we dwell upon them. Instead, focus on the divine as we are instructed in Romans 12:2, "Do not conform any longer to the pattern of this world, but be transformed by the renewing of your mind." Then as Romans 15:13 says, "May the God of hope fill you with all joy and peace as you trust in him, so that you may overflow with hope by the power of the Holy Spirit."

Scripture

Job 1:8-12:

Then the LORD said to Satan, "Have you considered my servant Job? There is no one on earth like him; he is blameless and upright, a man who fears God and shuns evil."

"Does Job fear God for nothing?" Satan replied. "Have you not put a hedge around him and his household and everything he has? You have blessed the work of his hands, so that his flocks and herds are spread throughout the land. [11] But now stretch out your hand and strike everything he has, and he will surely curse you to your face."

The LORD said to Satan, "Very well, then, everything he has is in your power, but on the man himself do not lay a finger."

Luke 12:22-31:

Then Jesus said to his disciples: "Therefore I tell you, do not worry about your life, what you will eat; or about your body, what you will wear. Life is more than food, and the body more than clothes. Consider the ravens: They do not sow or reap, they have no storeroom or barn; yet God feeds them. And how much more valuable you are than birds! Who of you by worrying can add a single hour to his life? Since you cannot do this very little thing, why do you worry about the rest?

"Consider how the lilies grow. They do not labor or spin. Yet I tell you, not even Solomon in all his splendor was dressed like one of these. If that is how God clothes the grass of the field, which is here today, and tomorrow is thrown into the fire, how much more will he clothe you, O you of little faith! And do not set your heart on what you will eat or drink; do not worry about it. For the pagan world runs after all such things, and your Father knows that you need them. But seek his kingdom, and these things will be given to you as well."

Galatians 5:22: But the fruit of the Spirit is love, joy, peace, patience, kindness, goodness, faithfulness, gentleness and self-control.

Ephesians 5:19: Speak to one another with psalms, hymns and spiritual songs. Sing and make music in your heart to the Lord.

Philippians 4:8: Finally, brothers and sisters, whatever is true, whatever is noble, whatever is right, whatever is pure, whatever is lovely, whatever is admirable— if anything is excellent or praiseworthy—think about such things.

Romans 12:2: Do not conform to the pattern of this world, but be transformed by the renewing of your mind.

Romans 15:13: May the God of hope fill you with all joy and peace as you trust in him, so that you may overflow with hope by the power of the Holy Spirit.

—20—

How the Holy Spirit
Guides Us: One

W hen I had just finished graduate school, I moved to
Florida to be with my parents who decided to get
a home there after my father retired. While living there,
I periodically visited a variety of churches. Although I
was brought up in the Catholic Church, having a Catholic
father and a Methodist mother allowed me to be more
open-minded about other denominations. Since the local
Catholic churches seemed so dry and dull, one Sunday I
decided to flip through the telephone book to find a nondenominational church I could try instead.

After finding the address of one that seemed suitable,
I hopped into my car and left. Usually able to navigate
my way in unfamiliar areas, I was disappointed when I
arrived where I thought it was located. Instead of finding
a church, I only found a sprinkling of homes among
empty lots. I proceeded to circle about the area, but I still
couldn't find this church. Frustration washed over me. It
was late and even if I did find it, the service would have

already begun by now. I just decided to go to a Catholic church since I still had time to get there for their next service.

Mass was just beginning as I entered St. Jude's Church. I quickly took a seat and viewed the congregation around me. The surrounding sea of white hair emphasized how different I was from them. I was also irritated by the formality and repetitiveness of the Mass. *Did anyone really think about what they were saying as they recited the formulated prayers, or were they just going through the motions?* Hardly anyone sang the songs, but for those who did, they sang with so little enthusiasm. Dissatisfaction seeped into my mind. Then, in the service, the Lord made it apparent to me that I should stop my criticism.

During the sermon, as the elderly priest seemed to drone on and on, my attention suddenly heightened when I heard him say, "The Catholic Church is not perfect, but it is a place to be." This strange statement in his sermon made me believe that the Holy Spirit was directing me to stop searching for another church. After all, I had just sought out a new place of worship that morning. Therefore, I vowed to stay affiliated with the Catholic Church.

It wasn't long after this episode that I ended up moving back to Pennsylvania to marry my high school sweetheart. Although David and I got married in the Catholic Church, we did not regularly attend Mass. However, two years later after having our first child, I was motivated to return to church to expose our child to a religious upbringing. My previous experience in Florida led me to seek out a Catholic Church to attend.

St. Steven's was a young and vibrant parish, located just down the road from our rented townhouse. As I began to attend Mass regularly, I came to respect the head priest, Father Ken. This clergyman was highly influenced by the Charismatic movement and enthusiastically promoted using the gifts of the Holy Spirit. He championed the baptism of the Spirit seminars, one of which I eventually attended, which was a pivotal event in my Christian walk.

Yet, my restlessness for another church resurfaced shortly after my spiritual baptism. I hungered for a more Bible-focused church than St. Steven's. However, since David was comfortable in the Catholic Church, I didn't push to go elsewhere. But after David's passing, I felt free to seek out a more Bible-focused denomination.

While entertaining these thoughts, I remember having a dream about three issues that were particularly challenging to me about Catholicism at the time. The following day was a Sunday and my children and I went to St. Steven's to attend Mass. Amazingly, during the priest's homily, he addressed all three of the concerns that had been in my dream. I believed once again the Holy Spirit was directing me to once again continue my alliance with the Catholic Church.

Not understanding why this church didn't promote reading the Bible more, I determined to implant Scripture any way I could into the church. I asked Clara, who overlooked the religious education department, if I could teach a CCD class. She told me that they had an opening for second grade that I could take and so I did.

That school year, I read Bible stories to the students, had them memorize weekly verses, and fashioned Bible-related crafts for them to do. However, I believed that the confinements of the Catholic traditions prevented me from producing any excitement for God in the children. Although discouraged, I continued to teach for another two years.

At the end of my third year of CCD, I once again came before the Lord beseeching, "Can I please leave now?" Whenever I prayed for answers in my life like in this situation, I believed the Holy Spirit answered with a voice that I would have to listen for inside. Sometimes, it just felt like I was just making up the response myself, but I eventually got better at discerning what I felt was the Holy Spirit and what was not. Anything that I heard that went against the Bible, I knew for sure it was not from God and ignored it. If I received conflicting input, I waited and kept seeking answers. If what I was seeking pertained to a weighty decision, I further attempted to verify the reply by reading the Word and additionally, seeking other Christians' counsel, and examining circumstances. It was by this method that I finally felt the Holy Spirit allowing me to leave the Catholic Church.

I was excited that I could finally leave and hopefully experience a more Biblically-based denomination. I resolved to go to a different church every Sunday until I discovered one where I felt my children could grow in Christ. While I sought out a new place of worship, I allowed my children to continue to attend St. Steven's. I figured they didn't need to be uprooted until we had a regular place to attend.

The nondenominational avenue was the most attractive to me. It seemed the longer a church had been in existence, the more entrenched the service became with man-made rules. I investigated various popular churches in the area. I figured if everyone else thought these churches were great, I might feel the same way.

The first congregation I explored was rather large. Seats were positioned in a semicircle around a stage. The extensive use of technology was surprising since the Catholic Church barely used any. Here, a massive screen displayed the words to the songs over various peaceful scenes, and lights flashed around. The service felt more like a production than something in which I was supposed to participate. Coming from a traditional background, I thought it bordered on sacrilege. The pastor donned a suit rather than the familiar gown and collar. The message was meaningful enough but then seemed overshadowed at its conclusion by pleas for attendance in numerous church programs. I chose to continue my search.

The next Sunday I went to a church that had a bit more formality to it. As I entered its foyer, a flood of people poured in around me. Then I heard someone greet me from behind, "Hi, Mary! How are you?" I turned and recognized a woman who had been a member of a Baptist church near my home. I had met her because our children had all been involved with the Christian children's club sponsored by her church.

"Did you leave Bible Baptist Church?" I asked.

"Yes. We wanted something different. We just love it here, and you will too. Everyone is so friendly," she boasted.

I sat with her and her family and examined the church. The building was an unimpressive, metal-paneled structure, but it was located on acres of beautiful, rolling farmland. The pastor was interesting enough, but the service seemed a little too similar to the formal proceedings of the Catholic church I had just left. I decided to keep looking.

The next Sunday, I went to a church that was only about a mile from our house. It was supposed to be a vibrant church but, when I entered, I suddenly felt very old. The members were mostly ten years younger than me and were busily herding their children to their various Sunday school classes. When the service started, music streamed from an electric keyboard from behind rather large Roman columns. Unfortunately, the regular pastor was not present, but I did not have enough motivation to return the next Sunday to hear him preach. It just did not feel like a match.

My next attempt brought me to a church with which I was somewhat familiar. Years ago my "Moms in Touch" group had met in the library of this Christian and Missionary Alliance church each week during the school year. I had always had a tender spot in my heart for the little church, as it seemed like something right out of the show *Little House on the Prairie*. Nestled into a hillside, it was so close to my home that I could probably have seen it from my house, if not for the trees in between.

As I made my way through the doors, another woman I knew greeted me. Although I did not sit with her, this greeting gave me a sense of familiarity in the unfamiliar. When I found a seat, I observed that there were only around hundred and fifty people in the pews. This was in sharp contrast to the roughly five thousand people who attended each of St. Steven's six Masses every weekend.

The service began with a string of songs. This was different from St. Steven's where the songs were interspersed throughout the service instead of being grouped all together. At the time, I was unfamiliar with the pieces played. Many of their verses were endlessly repeated, which seemed odd to me. Songs associated with the Catholic Church rarely repeated sections.

Numerous other differences from the Catholic Church service also were present. The various duties of the service were spread among the congregation instead of being led by a few official members. Young children collected the offering, and several men offered prayers from their seats in the pews. Again technology was present but, by this time, it was less flashy and I was beginning to feel more accustomed to it. The sermon was presented by a man named Pastor Dan, who again wore a suit instead of the more awe-inspiring robes with which I was familiar. His message was replete with scriptural references, and his message hit upon many issues relevant to my life. Warmth just seemed to radiate from this gathered body of Christ. I felt that this church was finally a good fit for our family.

When I arrived home, I informed my boys that we were going to change churches. "I have found the church that I believe will be good for our family. It is right down the road and called Faith Community Alliance Church," I shared.

"We don't want to leave St. Steven's," they whined.

"Just try it for me," I replied.

I practically had to drag them off to Faith Community the next Sunday. The complaining continued after the service. "They have a projector. What's up with that? . . . They keep singing the same verses over and over again... They don't have communion every Sunday... The priest wears a suit." I secretly smiled to myself, as I also had wrestled with some of the same objections.

With each passing Sunday, however, they became less critical. Eventually, they even grew eager to get ready, not wanting to be late for Sunday school. Peter joined a men's Bible study. John and Paul joined the youth group. John volunteered to operate the computer and projector during the services, while Paul became the church photographer. Additionally, Paul and I were inspired to get baptized by immersion. We all volunteered to help with Vacation Bible School in the summer, and I was compelled to teach a women's Bible study. With time, I even became the Director of Christian Education, which meant I was part of the governing board as well. Our spiritual growth during this time was immense.

After attending Faith Community for seven years, the Lord seemingly began to direct us to another church. Although Pastor Dan was still delivering interesting sermons, I was beginning to hunger for a different slant. Then around this time, Paul started to contemplate breaking up with a girl he had been dating from the church. Because the church was so small, it was going to be uncomfortable for him to continue to attend. Additionally, Pastor Dan elected to remove the pews from the sanctuary and replace them with moveable chairs. His thought was that it would be a solution to our lack of meeting space, since the chairs could be shifted about as needed. However, these new seats were treated with chemicals to make them resistant to staining. On the first Sunday we used them, waves of nausea from the chemicals began to pass over me and I started to feel dizzy. The following Sunday I positioned myself by an open window for relief, but I still felt queasy. Evaluating the fact I was had considered switching churches, my chemical sensitivity to the new chairs, and Paul's breakup, I asked the boys for their thoughts about switching churches. Neither of them objected, so I started looking again.

I had heard about another thriving congregation that had just started up recently. We visited Life Bridge Church and the pastor, although young, seemed extremely passionate and dependent upon the Lord. I didn't have the overwhelming peace that this was the perfect fit, but we continued to go anyway. I eventually volunteered to be a greeter and joined a small group that made me feel more connected. Slowly, over time, I began to feel the kinship that Christians usually experience when gathered together.

Although moving from one church to another was not always easy and often times frowned upon by others, I felt I had to obey what I believed the Holy Spirit was guiding me to do. In the middle of this transition, someone told me that they believed that if your church had a firm Biblical foundation, then you shouldn't leave. I didn't agree, as I saw the apostles always moving about and not settling in one church or area.

Just as each person is likened to a different part of the body, each church can excel at different aspect of Christianity. Some places of worship may excel at evangelism and others are gifted with educating the flock. One church may promote missions while another is talented at outreaching to the community. Another church may excel in the political arena. All together, the various churches carry out the particular mission that God has for them. Our Lord may call us to remain in one or to be constantly moving from one to another. The most important thing is that you are listening to what God wants you to do.

Reflecting back, I believe the Holy Spirit prompted me to change churches through circumstances, other Christians, prayer, a dream, and the Bible. How freeing to know that the Lord cares so much about us to work through the Holy Spirit to direct us in our Christian walk.

Scripture

2 Samuel 12:7-10 (Speaking through other Christians):

> Then Nathan said to David, "You are the man! This is what the LORD, the God of Israel, says: 'I anointed you king over Israel, and I delivered you from the hand of Saul. I gave your master's house to you, and your master's wives into your arms. I gave you all Israel and Judah. And if all this had been too little, I would have given you even more. Why did you despise the word of the LORD by doing what is evil in his eyes? You struck down Uriah the Hittite with the sword and took his wife to be your own. You killed him with the sword of the Ammonites. Now, therefore, the sword will never depart from your house, because you despised me and took the wife of Uriah the Hittite to be your own.'

Psalm 119:105 (God's Word as a guide): Your word is a lamp for my feet, a light for my path.

Isaiah 30:21 (Holy Spirit's voice): Whether you turn to the right or to the left, your ears will hear a voice behind you, saying, "This is the way; walk in it."

Matthew 1:20 (Speaking through dreams): But after he had considered this, an angel of the Lord appeared to him in a dream and said, "Joseph son of David, do not be afraid to take Mary home as your wife, because what is conceived in her is from the Holy Spirit."

Acts 16:6-7 (Holy Spirit intervening): Paul and his companions traveled throughout the region of Phrygia and Galatia, having been kept by the Holy Spirit from preaching the word in the province of Asia. When they came to the border of Mysia, they tried to enter Bithynia, but the Spirit of Jesus would not allow them to.

—21—

Crying Out to God in Prayer

S ince David's death, the chore of mowing the lawn had fallen to me. During the summer, I usually passed the task on to my boys but, during the school year, it was difficult for them to find a time to do it. After a day of school, they whined they were too tired since they had to get up early and were very busy. I never wanted them to cut the grass on Sunday, thinking it was breaking God's law of rest on the Sabbath. That left only Saturdays for accomplishing this chore.

Normally, I would have enjoyed cutting grass because I liked being outside, and it would have provided me with some form of exercise. However, our backyard was like a ski slope, which required a great deal of strength to keep the lawn mower steady while weaving back and forth against the steep incline. Since I had already undergone two hernia surgeries, I was reluctant to engage in any activity that might precipitate another one. I was especially hesitant because, after my last surgery, the doctor had informed me that I still had another hernia around my belly button. Although he had told me not to worry about it, I was hesitant to do any activity that might aggravate it.

This particular fall day was sunny, unlike the forecast for the remainder of the week, which was for rain. Since today was Thursday, I knew that if I did not cut the lawn now, I would have to look at an overgrown yard for the next week. I decided I really wanted the lawn done. I could probably cut it just this one time without hurting myself too much. I got out the lawn mower and started to cut the grass. Once finished, I was happy that the lawn was done and that I felt little discomfort.

The next day, while admiring my well-kept yard, I noticed a dead branch hanging down from one of the trees in my backyard. I wanted to cut it off, so I got a handsaw from the garage and began hacking away at the branch. My neighbor, who lived behind me and loved to tend to his yard, spied my lame attempt at removing the limb. He excitedly offered to cut the branch for me, so I gladly accepted. He came over and fired up his chainsaw and sliced off the offending branch with ease. Satisfied with this work, he eyed the rest of my trees and volunteered to thin out some more of the low-hanging limbs that made cutting the grass difficult. I gratefully accepted his offer, so he proceeded to cut off these branches as well. When he finished, I thanked him, and he immediately excused himself and went back to his home. I looked around the yard—the trees looked great, but tree branches blanketed half of my backyard.

The only place I could think of disposing of all these branches was in the large wooded area across the street behind another neighbor's house. After getting that neighbor's permission to put the branches there, I enlisted the help of my youngest son, who had just gotten off the school bus. We began the laborious task of dragging all the tree limbs up the hill of my backyard, over my front yard, across the street, and up another hill into the woods. The boughs were unwieldy, but with much effort, we slowly removed them from our yard.

Between cutting the grass the day before and now removing the branches, I was in pain by the evening. My abdomen really hurt, and I feared I had exacerbated my hernia and would once again need surgery.

Full of dread, I called my primary care doctor the next day and made an appointment with the physician's assistant. After looking me over, she confirmed my fears and asked if I had a particular surgeon in mind to perform the operation. I selected a doctor who had done surgery on my daughter Anna the previous year for a horseback riding accident.

When this surgeon examined me, he also agreed that I had a hernia and that it needed to be repaired by surgery. He explained that he would make a vertical incision and use a mesh patch to repair the hernia during the procedure. I was glad he was going to use a mesh patch since my previous two hernia surgeries included them. He gave me orders to have blood work and an EKG done prior to surgery. Additionally, he directed me to schedule a CT scan so he could pinpoint the exact location of the hernia, if possible.

Thinking about my upcoming surgery, I remembered a couple of months earlier viewing a story on the television about a woman who had undergone an unsuccessful abdominal operation. The doctor had used a vertical cut, which had resulted in a mountain-like scar, with the peak at the point of the incision. Her torso looked deformed, and she was still experiencing a great deal of pain. Even though there are always horror stories about operations, I couldn't help but wonder why my doctor preferred a vertical cut over the other option of a horizontal cut.

Soon afterward, while attending one of John's cross-country meets, I discussed my upcoming surgery with another mother there. By coincidence, her husband had undergone a hernia operation performed by this same surgeon. She confided that her husband felt pulling and a lot of discomfort afterward. When he complained to the doctor, the doctor was unsympathetic and unwilling to do anything further to alleviate the situation. Additionally, she shared that this doctor had not used mesh in the repair procedure.

When the doctor had spoken with me earlier, he confirmed that he was going to use mesh. However, I was worried that he would decide to not use mesh in my surgery and that I, too, would have discomfort afterwards. Concern washed over me as I listened to her comments, but I chose to dismiss them. Perhaps he had perfected his technique or maybe the procedure was different for men.

Three days before my surgery, the doctor's office called to request additional blood work. They wanted to determine my blood type in order to have a supply ready in case it became necessary. Maybe this was just a standard preoperative procedure that they had overlooked when I had my original blood work performed, but it unnerved me. I worried that they had seen something in my tests that prompted them to suggest this extra measure. Furthermore, if I had been informed of this need earlier, I could have donated my own blood. I recalled that when Peter received additional blood after his car accident, there seemed to be some risk involved. Now, I might have to face those same uncertainties.

The night before the surgery, I was extremely unsettled. I wanted to cancel the procedure as my abdomen felt fine right now. I thought about the television story of the vertical cut that created a distorted abdomen. I reflected upon the unsatisfactory results of my friend's husband's surgery. I wondered why I had been called in for more blood work. Despite all my misgivings, I lacked the courage to call the hospital and say, *"Oh, I've changed my mind. I don't want to have this surgery."*

Since I felt helpless to do anything, I determined to offer up a prayer to God. I recently had read a book named, *The Power of Crying Out*, about prayers that get answered swiftly. It claimed that prayers that are offered with passion and spoken out loud get answered more quickly than those where we don't think they will be heard or we give little thought to them. As an example, it referred to the Israelites and many others in the Old Testament and how they didn't just pray, but they cried out to the Lord.[1]

When I looked up this occurrence in the Bible, I found that it was true. They would plead fervently before the Lord and He would immediately respond. I was desperate, so I decided that I would try this technique.

Wanting to be by myself, I went up to my bedroom and shut the door. I got down on my knees and raised my arms to heaven. I literally cried aloud, "Lord! I don't feel like I should be going through with this surgery. You know my personality. You know I'm unable to back out now. You are the one who made me the way I am. I'm putting this surgery into Your hands."

I thought I would instantly feel at peace, but my anxiety persisted. I later went to bed and tried to sleep, but my uneasiness still lingered. I berated myself for my lack of faith.

The next morning, I nervously got ready to go. My daughter drove me to the hospital. Normally, she would have been away at college, but a freak hurricane had passed through her college town. Since they didn't have any power, the university had sent all the students home for the past five days. Anna was planning on driving back to school after I got out of surgery.

I still felt uneasy about the procedure, but I had prayed. I was leaving this in God's hands. Whatever was going to happen was going to happen. I methodically moved through the steps toward the surgery, feeling like a lamb heading toward slaughter.

Shortly after I arrived at the hospital, Dan, the pastor at the church I was currently attending, showed up to pray over the proceedings. We bowed our heads while sitting in the waiting room. He prayed for wisdom for the doctor and for a rapid recovery. Soon after we finished, I was called back to get prepared for surgery.

"Please sign this paper, and then I'll take you back to get changed," the nurse prompted. I perused the sheet and I was surprised by something it said. The document stated that the doctor had the option of using or not using the mesh patch. *Ugh...He told me that he was going to use mesh!* This concerned me, but not wanting to be confrontational, I signed the paper. I prayed once again that God was keeping His hand on the circumstances.

The nurse continued preparing me for surgery. "Change into this gown, and place your clothes into this locker. Put this cap on, and tuck your hair into it. Here are some warm socks for your feet."

When I had accomplished everything she directed me to do, she led me back to the preoperative area. She sat me in a rather large, leather chair and then proceeded to insert an IV into one of the veins of my hand. Years ago it had been determined that I had mitral valve prolapse, which required me to receive antibiotics before undergoing any type of surgery.

By a quarter to ten, I was fully prepared and ready for the surgery, which was scheduled for ten o'clock. My daughter was brought back to sit with me until the doctor arrived. I aimlessly chatted with the nurse about the joys of raising teenagers.

Ten o'clock came and went. At ten thirty, I began to wonder if I had prayed the doctor into a car accident. Finally, at eleven o'clock, the doctor came bursting through the pre-op door. There was quickness to his gait. I called out to him since he had not yet seen me. Veering from his determined direction, he strode to my side. Appearing flustered, he queried, "Why are you here today?"

"I had abdominal pain, and you diagnosed me with a hernia," I replied.

"Stand up and let me feel your abdomen," he instructed. He pressed various areas of my midsection and then quickly announced, "I misdiagnosed you. You just strained some muscles. I'm canceling your surgery."

I was astonished! I couldn't believe that I was escaping surgery! After the nurse removed my IV, I darted back to the changing area and quickly dressed in my regular clothes. I wanted to get out of there as fast as I could before they changed their minds.

I went home praising God for getting me out of the surgery and since then, I have not experienced any further problems with my abdomen. I truly believe that my passionately crying out to God and turning the whole situation over to Him allowed me to have such a positive outcome.

Scripture

Exodus 2:23 (Italics added): During that long period, the king of Egypt died. The *Israelites groaned in their slavery and cried out*, and their cry for help because of their slavery went up to God. God heard their groaning and he remembered his covenant with Abraham, with Isaac and with Jacob.

Exodus 8:12-13 (Italics added): After Moses and Aaron left Pharaoh, *Moses cried out to the LORD* about the frogs he had brought on Pharaoh. And the LORD did what Moses asked. The frogs died in the houses, in the courtyards and in the fields.

Numbers 20:15-16 (Italics added): "Our forefathers went down into Egypt, and we lived there many years. The Egyptians mistreated us and our fathers, *but when we cried out* to the Lord, he heard our cry and sent an angel and brought us out of Egypt."

Judges 3:15 (Italics added): Again the *Israelites cried out to the LORD*, and he gave them a deliverer—Ehud, a left-handed man, the son of Gera the Benjamite. The Israelites sent him with tribute to Eglon king of Moab.

Judges 6:7-8, 14 (Italics and parentheses content added): When the *Israelites cried out to the LORD* because of Midian, he sent them a prophet, who said, "This is what the LORD, the God of Israel, says: I brought you up out of Egypt, out of the land of slavery.

The LORD turned to him (Gideon) and said, "Go in the strength you have and save Israel out of Midian's hand. Am I not sending you?"

Judges 15:18-19 (Italics added): Because he was very thirsty, *he cried out to the LORD*, "You have given your servant this great victory. Must I now die of thirst and fall into the hands of the uncircumcised?" Then God opened up the hollow place in Lehi, and water came out of it. When Samson drank, his strength returned and he revived. So the spring was called En Hakkore, and it is still there in Lehi.

1 Samuel 12:8 (Italics added): After Jacob entered Egypt, *they cried to the LORD* for help, and the LORD sent Moses and Aaron, who brought your ancestors out of Egypt and settled them in this place.

1 Kings 17:20-22 (Italics added): Then *he cried out* to the LORD, "LORD my God, have you brought tragedy even on this widow I am staying with, by causing her son to die?" Then he stretched himself out on the boy three times and cried out to the LORD, "LORD my God, let this boy's life return to him!"

The LORD heard Elijah's cry, and the boy's life returned to him, and he lived.

Praising God in All Things

I always fretted when I had to make the drive to the university that my daughter attended. First, I had to navigate the always-under-construction Pennsylvania Turnpike. Then, I had to either meander over two-lane back roads or navigate the heavily traveled, eight-lane highways around Washington, D.C. However, she was now graduating from college, and I did not want to miss her commencement.

I knew I would be worn out if I left Saturday morning for the preliminary candlelight procession scheduled for later that evening, so I decided to leave on Friday instead. That way, I thought, I could help Anna pack her things during the day on Saturday. This would allow us to immediately leave after the graduation ceremony scheduled for Sunday afternoon.

John and Paul complained about going. "Please don't make us go," they whined, dedicated to their schoolwork. "If we miss school on Friday, we will have to make up a lot of work. What are we going to do there all weekend, anyway?"

This was one of those parenting battles that I could not muster the energy to fight. Peter was already going, driving from his college. If I forced my two younger boys to go, I feared they would dampen the celebration for the rest of us. "All right, you can stay home, but make sure you go to church on Sunday," I conceded. "I will have Pastor Dan's family take you."

The Wednesday before I was to leave, I was sitting in a chair in my living room when a sharp pain shot above my right breast. As it continued, I wondered what it could be. *Was it just a passing pain, or did it signal something more serious? Should I be concerned?*

By evening, the pain had traveled to under my armpit, and by morning it had progressed to my back. I considered going to the doctor, but decided to try to ignore it.

At eight thirty that morning, my phone rang. "Hi, how are you?" my sister inquired.

"I'm okay, but I have this strange pain that started yesterday," I shared with her. My sister, who normally suggests avoiding doctors at all costs, encouraged me to have it checked out before making my big trip. I decided that was probably wise advice, so I made an appointment with my doctor and went to his office later that afternoon.

When I was called back to a room, the nurse took my blood pressure and asked, "Why are you here today?" I explained my problem to her. She wrote down the symptoms and told me the physician's assistant would be coming soon.

When the specialist arrived, she examined me and said," It sounds like you have shingles. The pain is running along the nerve line, and it is only on one side." As she scrutinized my torso, she additionally pointed out, "See, here is a raised bump on your breast that looks like a pock."

Immediately I flashed back to when my husband he had shingles. When Anna was just two weeks old, David contracted such an intense case that he had to be hospitalized. He continued to suffer from residual pain in his scalp for the rest of his life. Now, I was seemingly diagnosed with the same dreadful ailment, and I was supposed to be driving six hours to be at Anna's graduation in two days.

"Is it possible that it's something else?" I pleaded.

"Well, have you done anything strenuous lately?" the physician's assistant inquired.

"I moved some furniture last Saturday." I brightened with the thought that it could be a reason for the pain instead of shingles. It had been five days earlier, but I was desperate for an alternate diagnosis.

"There is a slight chance it could be just a pulled muscle, and the pock could be just a skin deformity," she replied. Then she continued, "There isn't anything I can give you to prevent shingles, but I can prescribe medicine to lessen the intensity and duration of the outbreak. Take it as soon as you begin to break out in more pocks. I can give you some muscle relaxants if you think it is due to a pulled muscle though."

After getting packets of the prescribed drugs and checking out, I made my way to my car. I contemplated all the previous struggles I had faced in recent years. I plopped down in the front seat and began praying to God. "Lord, I guess this is another stressful situation you are letting me endure. I know nothing can touch me that hasn't first passed through your hands. You have allowed this, for whatever reason. I will praise you for this latest trial because it must be for my good."

Normally, I would not have prayed in this manner, but I remembered how Job stated we should accept not only the good from God but also bad. Somehow, I translated it into my mind that we should appreciate everything that befalls us—good or bad—so this thought was fresh in my mind.

Unsure whether I had shingles or had just a pulled muscle, I optimistically chose to take the muscle-relaxing medicine. I then delayed leaving for Anna's graduation until Saturday to give myself more time to see if this pain truly was going to develop into shingles. If I was going to break out into a full-blown case of contagious pocks, it might be best to stay home. However, if my symptoms failed to progress, then possibly I could attempt the trip.

When I woke up Friday morning, I still felt some discomfort, but it seemed to have lessened. I decided to proceed with the trip and began to busy myself with preparations to leave. Since I was now leaving when John and Paul wouldn't have to miss school, I made up my mind to make John and Paul accompany me in case my situation deteriorated and I needed help. I telephoned my pastor's wife, Linda, and informed her of our change of plans so she would know that she did not have to pick them up for church on Sunday. I also shared with her about the possibility that I had shingles, and she told me that she and her family would pray.

On Saturday, the pain was scarcely noticeable as I drove. Additionally, the usual muscle stiffness I experience when sitting in the car for such a long period of time was absent, probably because of the residual muscle relaxants in my system.

The weekend was wonderful with the entire family being present for Anna's graduation. I was so proud of all the hard work Anna had done over the past years, especially considering all the difficulties she faced as part of our family and individually. Additionally, my pain was gone and no additional pocks presented themselves.

After returning home, since I still was feeling good, I was curious if the pock that the physician had spotted was still present. If it was, then my pain could have truly been from a strained muscle but, if it wasn't, then maybe the Lord had intervened and healed me. I looked down and saw that particular area was now completely smooth, with no trace of a bump.

While I can't confirm that I had shingles and that I was cured, I again thanked God for my not having an outbreak. I was thankful my entire family was able to attend Anna's graduation as well. I wondered if praising God had allowed me to avoid getting the disease. Regardless, it encouraged me to always thank God for all things in my life—both pleasant and challenging. Doing so really displays our trust in God's hand in our lives. Then possibly, He will even reward our faithfulness.

Scripture

Job 2:10: He replied, "You are talking like a foolish woman. Shall we accept good from God, and not trouble?" In all this, Job did not sin in what he said.

1Thessalonians 5:16-18 (Italics added): Be joyful always, pray continually, give thanks in *all circumstances*; for this is God's will for you in Christ Jesus.

—23—

The Power in Jesus' Name

W hat was that ringing? Somewhere in my con-
sciousness I could hear it, but could not formulate
in my mind what it was. Then almost automatically, my
hand reached for the phone on the nightstand. I glanced
at the clock as I picked up the receiver. It was three thirty
in the morning.

The husky man's voice on the other end forcibly
requested, "Can I speak with Mr. Kaczynski?" Disbelief
washed over me. *Why would someone—and in the middle
of the night, no less—be asking for my husband, who had
passed away more than eight years ago?* I suspected that
this person knew "Mr. Kaczynski" was not available and
just desired to harass me. I, therefore, didn't respond.

More aggressively, the man, knowing that I was on
the line, persisted with his demand two additional times.
"Where is Mr. Kaczynski?" I still did not answer. My
instinct was to hang up the phone, so I did.

181

The phone immediately rang again. It seemed the caller was not going to be so easily deterred. I picked up the receiver. "Don't hang up on me!" he barked.

At that moment I pictured Jesus and His angels surrounding and protecting me. With this vision now in my head, I answered defiantly, "I'm not afraid of you," and slammed the receiver to the cradle once again.

The phone rang a third time. I snatched up the receiver only to hear him threaten, "If you hang up again, I know where you live, and I'll come over."

"You just come on over and see what you find!" I spouted and once again forcibly returned the phone to its cradle. *What had I just said?*

I felt God would protect me, but yet my confidence shocked me. Then a rush of fear permeated my body. *Did he really know where I lived? Would he come over?* I dialed 911.

"A man just made a threatening phone call to me," I explained.

"What do you want us to do?" the woman retorted.

"I thought maybe you could have someone drive by my house to make sure there weren't any suspicious cars in my neighborhood," I informed her with irritation.

"All right," she replied.

I turned off the ringer to my phone, but now I was fully awake. I lay very quietly in my bed and listened for any vehicles moving up or down my street, but I never heard any. I called out to the Lord and pictured angels surrounding my house and took comfort in that.

I never heard any police cars go by, but I relied upon the power of Christ to keep me safe. The morning light eventually arrived without further incident. However, I was on edge for the next few nights. I continually had to remind myself that the Lord would protect me as I called upon His Name. He honored my pleas as I never did receive any more threatening calls.

I was confident that God would protect me because I had heard of many stories in the past where He intervened on behalf of someone in trouble. I specifically thought back about a story about a woman who had a man threaten to come over to her house to do her harm. She prayed to Jesus to protect her and the man never arrived. Sometime later, this would-be-attacker had the occasion to ask the woman concerning that night. He claimed that he had come to her house, but then left because he saw men guarding her house, most of them being positioned upon the roof. He asked her who they were. The woman was shocked to hear this, as she was unaware that anyone was protecting her. She surmised that they must have been angels. I thought if it worked for her, it could work for me.

I later heard that when we offer up prayers, we should specifically use Jesus' name. A story I heard on the radio spoke of a girl who had allowed a man to drive her home. As they neared her driveway, the man did not stop but drove right past it. The girl informed the man that he had gone too far, but he did not answer. The girl grew frightened because the road they were traveling upon led to a desolate area. She recalled a recent sermon about how there is power in Jesus' name when we call upon him in difficult circumstances, so she did. After doing this, the driver suddenly turned the car around and dropped her off at her house.

A few years later, I saw a news story on television about a store owner in Texas who defiantly commanded a would-be robber to leave her store in the name of Jesus.

When he continued to make demands, she still refused and adamantly said, "In the name of Jesus, I command you to get out of my store!" He ended up leaving without any money and no one got hurt.[1] The whole incident was captured on the store's security camera.[2]

The reason we should cover our prayers in Jesus' name is found in Matthew 28:18. After Jesus died on the cross, He was resurrected and then given all authority in heaven and on earth. This power is often manifested by merely drawing upon Jesus' name as it says in Philippians 2:9-10, "Therefore, God exalted him to the highest place and gave him the name that is above every name, that at the name of Jesus every knee should bow, in heaven and on earth and under the earth." Psalm 8:1, 103:1, 113:1-3, and 148:13 additionally tell us to glorify Jesus' name.

A name reflects one's character, reputation, and importance. A good name is one of a person's most valuable possessions. Proverbs 22:1 states, "A good name is more desirable than great riches; to be esteemed is better than silver or gold." Ecclesiastes 7:1a also shares how valuable a name is when it says, "A good name is better than fine perfume." [3]

Sometimes others can receive benefits when they come using the name of someone else. For example, one of the president's children could enjoy certain favors just by being related to him. Even though they did not personally earn those advantages, they still can receive them because they are associated to the one who has earned those benefits.

When Jesus died on the cross, He enabled all believers to become adopted sons and daughters of God. As children of God, when we profess Jesus' name, we can draw upon His power to help, heal, renew, and comfort us and others in our lives. We do not claim we have authority in ourselves but are using Jesus' power. However, there are times when we call upon Jesus' name for help and nothing appears to happen. There are a variety of reasons for this occurring.

Firstly, using this spiritual weapon is reserved only for believers and those followers must have a strong bond to the Lord. John 15:1-8 compares a grapevine to the type of relationship we need with our Heavenly Father. God is pictured as the life-giving vine and His worshippers as the branches. Only when the branches remain connected to the vine, do they have access to the benefits of the vine.[4] Furthermore, most of the verses in the Bible that claim that the Lord will answer our petitions have some sort of attachment with it. John 15:7 states, "If you remain in me and my words remain in you, ask whatever you wish, and it will be given you." Psalm 37:4 promises that if you, "delight yourself in the Lord and he will give you the desires of your heart." Then 1 John 3:21-22 says, "Dear friends, if our hearts do not condemn us, we have confidence before God and receive from him anything we ask, because we obey his commands and do what pleases him."

In fact, if a nonbeliever attempts to petition our Lord to fend off evil by using the Name of Jesus, they may find themselves facing much trouble, as exposed in Acts 19:13-17. It discloses, "Some Jews who went around driving out evil spirits tried to invoke the name of the Lord Jesus over those who were demon-possessed. They would say, 'In the name of the Jesus, whom Paul preaches, I command you to come out.' Seven sons of Sceva, a Jewish chief priest, were doing this. One day the evil spirit answered them, 'Jesus I know, and Paul I know about, but who are you?' Then the man who had the evil spirit jumped on them and overpowered them all. He gave them such a beating that they ran out of the house naked and bleeding. When this became known to the Jews and Greeks living in Ephesus, they were all seized with fear, and the name of the Lord Jesus was held in high honor." Thus, calling upon the Name of Jesus without first having a bond with Him can expose one to harm.[5]

Secondly, sin in our lives can prevent God from acting when we call on His name. First Peter 3:7 specifically points out that the prayers of a man will be hindered if he treats his wife harshly. Luke 18:10-14 shares a story about a man being arrogant and not having his prayers answered. James 4:3 claims that wrong motives, such as just wanting things for your pleasure, will prevent prayers from being heard.

Thirdly, being greedy may interfere with our prayers being answered. Proverbs 21:13 says that, "If a man shuts his ears to the cry of the poor, he too will cry out and not be answered." Giving, on the other hand, seems to encourage God to act. Acts 10:31 states that Cornelius prayers were heard because of the gifts he gave to the poor.[6]

Fourthly, the Lord examines our faith before answering our pleas. Do we truly believe that by crying out to the Lord He will hear us and act, or do we have little hope of Him answering us? In Mark 6:5, we observe that even Jesus had difficulty accomplishing miracles in His hometown. The people there did not believe that He was able to accomplish the miracles and so he did not do that many miraculous signs there.

Fifthly and finally, it would be impossible for God to answer everyone's requests, as many would be in conflict with each other or with His will. Additionally, if God answered every petition, it would then be mankind who was in control of the world and not God. However, God has a purpose for everyone, and sometimes that purpose is accomplished by allowing people to have difficulties.

Jesus is ultimately in control and knows the entire picture. Unbeknownst to us, granting what we desire short-term may in the long-term may be harmful to us. Therefore, we should always seek God's will for a situation and be at peace for whatever unfolds.[7]

Gordon Richards, in an article about entitled, "The Name of Jesus," relays a story about himself in a small town in Africa when he needed to make a phone call. There were two pay phones beside each other. One did not work, and there was a long line for the other phone. Mr. Richards went to the one that was not working and prayed over it saying, "In the name of Jesus start working." The phone immediately had service.

The next time this man was in this same town, the problematic phone was again not working. However, this time, he felt like the Lord did not want him to pray over it. Instead, he had to take some time to search for another one to use. While he was looking for an alternative telephone, a very bad accident happened on the highway where one of the men involved lost both of his legs. He figured that spending more time to find the other phone had prevented him from being involved in that accident. He would have been on that road at that time if the broken phone would have started to work again. When Mr. Richards returned to the United States, his family remembered that date and had felt that he had been in grave danger during on that particular day and prayed for his safety.[8]

It is clear that specifically calling on Jesus' name is especially powerful, and as adopted sons and daughters of God, we are free to call upon His name to help us in our time of need. Then we should allow God to be God and accept whatever way He chooses to answer.

Scripture

Name of the Lord

Matthew 28:18: Then Jesus came to them and said, "All authority in heaven and on earth has been given to me."

Philippians 2:9-10: Therefore God exalted him to the highest place and gave him the name that is above every name, that at the name of Jesus every knee should bow, in heaven and on earth and under the earth.

Psalm 8:1a: O LORD our Lord, how excellent is thy name in all the earth!

Psalm 103:1: Praise the LORD, O my soul; all my inmost being, praise his holy name.

Psalm 113:1-3: Praise the LORD. Praise, O servants of the LORD, praise the name of the LORD. Let the name of the LORD be praised, both now and forevermore. From the rising of the sun to the place where it sets, the name of the LORD is to be praised.

Psalm 148:13a: Let them praise the name of the LORD: for his name alone is exalted.

Ask in the Name of Jesus

John 14:14: You may ask me for anything in my name, and I will do it.

John 16:23-24: "In that day you will no longer ask me anything. I tell you the truth, my Father will give you whatever you ask in my name. Until now you have not asked for anything in my name. Ask and you will receive, and your joy will be complete."

Acts 2:21: "And everyone who calls on the name of the Lord will be saved."

Aids to prayer being answered

Acts 10:31: "And said, 'Cornelius, God has heard your prayer and remembered your gifts to the poor.'"

Prayers not being answered

Proverbs 21:13: If a man shuts his ears to the cry of the poor, he too will cry out and not be answered.

Mark 6:5-6: He could not do any miracles there, except lay his hands on a few sick people and heal them. And he was amazed at their lack of faith.

Luke 18:10-14:

"Two men went up to the temple to pray, one a Pharisee and the other a tax collector. The Pharisee stood up and prayed about himself: 'God, I thank you that I am not like other men—robbers, evildoers, adulterers—or even like this tax collector. I fast twice a week and give a tenth of all I get.' "But the tax collector stood at a distance. He would not even look up to heaven, but beat his breast and said, 'God, have mercy on me, a sinner.' "I tell you that this man, rather than the other, went home justified before God. For everyone who exalts himself will be humbled, and he who humbles himself will be exalted."

James 4:3: When you ask, you do not receive, because you ask with wrong motives, that you may spend what you get on your pleasures.

1 Peter 3:7: Husbands, in the same way be considerate as you live with your wives, and treat them with respect as the weaker partner and as heirs with you of the gracious gift of life, so that nothing will hinder your prayers.

God's Permissive Will

After David died, I missed him deeply. Yet I could not wallow in my grief as I had four kids to raise. I was often forced back into reality. "Mommy, do I have clean socks? . . . I need a snack for school on Friday... Mommy, he hit me!" While I still had the responsibilities of parenting four children, the desire for a man in my life persistently surfaced. As Paul, John, Peter, and Anna vied for my attention, my mind often daydreamed about having someone with whom to share my life.

The first man to enter my life came about ten months after David passed away. It was during this time that Anna had expressed interest in going to World Youth Day, a gathering of Catholic youth in Rome from all over the world. Anyone interested in going was required to attend a series of meetings. During the first of such gatherings, I looked around the room and saw a man that piqued my interest. *Hmm, he's nice and tall and appears to be single.* He must have had a child going to the World Youth Day as well.

At the next meeting, I discovered that this man, who was named Bob, was in fact single and had divorced over twenty years ago. He did not have children, but was accompanying the group as a chaperone. Bob and I eventually got to know each other and began to date.

It didn't take long for my daughter to make known her feelings about this new man in my life. "Mom, I don't like Bob," she told me constantly. Understandably, it was difficult for her. She had lost her father not long ago, and Bob was very different from her father.

I usually tended to succumb to my children's desires, but this time was different. As I mentioned earlier, not long after Bob and I began to get acquainted, my seven-year-old son was diagnosed with Hodgkin's disease. I desperately needed support to deal with all the pressures of being single and having a child with cancer. I had wonderful neighbors, but they had their own spouses and their own lives and my parents and siblings lived far away in Florida. So despite Anna's objections, I continued to see Bob.

"Honey, I'm sorry, but either you put up with him or you will have to commit me to an insane asylum," I often said in an attempt to justify my behavior.

Bob and I dated for six months, but the tension between my children's desires and my desire for male companionship plagued me. I attempted to break it off once, but then we continued to see each other. We dated several more months until I believed the stress began to express itself physically, as I started to bleed without cause. I went to a doctor who suggested I get a colonoscopy. I did and, fortunately, the results came back negative for cancer.

Feeling this ailment was truly from all the pressure I was under, I was determined to break off my relationship with Bob this time and did. The next day, my bleeding promptly ceased. I vowed to refrain from dating for at least the next couple of years in an effort to not upset my children.

Two years later though, I began to feel sorry for myself about my plight and decided to plead my case before the Lord. "Lord, I didn't put myself in this situation. Please send someone into my life," I directed. I even added a few stipulations about any possible man that the Lord might send. However, if this wasn't what the Lord wanted for me, I also offered, "Or, Lord, let me teach at a small Christian college." I figured that if it was not God's will for a man to be in my life at this time, then teaching could distract me from my singleness.

This alternate prayer of teaching at the college level was rather bold, since I had not taught high school in seventeen years. I possessed only a master's degree, and most college-level positions preferred someone with a doctorate. However, ever since my days as a graduate assistant, I had envisioned myself as an instructor at the college level. After marrying and having children, I began to doubt it would ever occur. I loved being a full-time wife and mother, but now that my husband was gone, I resurrected this dream.

Right after sending up this plea, I paged through some singles magazines, published by Focus on the Family that my friend, Sandy, had given me. She was a fellow widow that I had met through a young widows and widowers group. One of the magazines had an article about safe Christian matchmaking sites on the Internet. It caught my interest. From the comfort of my home, I could explore prospective men who professed to be Christian. I decided to try it out in hopes of finding someone.

I logged onto one of the three sites listed. After completing an exhaustive questionnaire, I moved to the section that asked me to describe the type of person I would like to meet. I relayed my desires. "I would like to meet a Christian widower who has children," I typed.

I had reasons for my stipulations, of course. Meeting someone who was a Christian was essential as it is the only requirement given in the Bible as to what a follower of Christ needs to have in a spouse. Second Corinthians 6:14 warns against being "unequally yoked" in a relationship. This made sense to me because unless someone was a Christian, he would always be at odds with my beliefs. I preferred a widower so I wouldn't have to compete with another woman from a previous marriage. Additionally, I thought that if the man had children of his own, he would be more sensitive to making sacrifices needed in dealing with having kids. Then, weary from the plethora of questions, I hit '*submit*' and went to bed.

The next morning, I visited the site again and received an announcement. "You have mail." One of the responses was from a man who lived about three hours away. He was widowed, with two boys aged nine and eleven. He was a professor with a small Christian college and seemed attractive enough from his picture.

I responded to his message, and soon we began emailing daily back and forth. As I got to know the professor, I investigated the institution where he taught. I discovered that it offered family and consumer sciences, my field of expertise. This shocked me, as not many colleges still offered this major. I wondered what the chances of finding such a match were.

After a month of emailing back and forth, he finally asked, "Do you want to meet?"

"I guess so. Where?" I replied hesitantly. Meeting was not an easy thing to plan, since we both had young children that still needed adult supervision.

"Let's meet for lunch while the kids are in school. Cleveland is about halfway between us. I'll find a restaurant there," he suggested.

"All right," I agreed.

We met up and had a fine time, but after meeting him, I questioned whether we were a good match. He was shorter than I was, which was bothersome, however shallow of me. At his Christian college, he also was part of an extremely conservative environment with many rules, such as no drinking whatsoever. This had to be adhered to or his job could be jeopardized. On the other hand, he was so very close to what I desired and, at this point, I was desperately craving to be in a relationship. Since our lunch date was pleasant enough, we agreed to keep communicating and meeting whenever we could.

It felt so good to have someone in this world who was concerned about me, yet an underlying sense of restlessness continually plagued me. *Was he really what I was looking for?* If we moved forward in this relationship, I would have to take my children out of their school, where they were doing so well. My kids would also have to adjust to additional siblings that were culturally very different from them. It was not an easy decision to make and came to a head nine months later.

"Let's get married," the professor offered.

"That sounds tempting, but I can't. Anna is so close to graduating from high school. After she graduates, then we can do it," I hedged, trying to evade the offer. Months passed and Anna graduated from high school.

The professor asked again. My reply was much the same. "I can't. Peter is just a year from graduating from high school now. After he graduates, then I can move since John and Paul will just be entering high school. Then would be a better time," I said.

My uneasiness about the relationship had me constantly seeking the Lord's will in this matter. I prayed, "God, is this the man I should marry?" On one occasion, I prayed that if we were not meant to be together, the professor would end it.

In our very next conversation, I used the word '*darn.*'

"Do you always use that word?" he questioned.

"Sometimes, why?" I replied.

He responded, "We never use that word. We consider it a swear word."

This almost insignificant issue to me bothered him so much that he broke off the relationship. I thought it was bizarre to end a relationship over what I considered a harmless word. I concluded that the Lord must have motivated him to do so.

However, several months later, he called again, desiring to get back together. I agreed to do so because I missed him. My reluctance to formally commit to him still persisted, though. I decided to introduce him to my friends to garner their opinions of him. None of them responded positively, probably because I had shared about why he had broken up with me previously. Still, the professor pushed to get married and I kept trying to elude his proposal.

Then, the professor forwarded an email to me about an announcement of a job opening as an instructor in the family and consumer sciences department at the college where he taught. The position was ideal. Not only was it at an institution where I could teach courses in my field from a religious perspective, but the program offered had a more traditional flair, which I preferred. Even more amazing, the position was part-time, which would allow me time to attend to my children's needs.

I was truly amazed how, after I prayed to meet a Christian widower with children or to teach at a small Christian college, I had met the professor the next day and now I had a possible opportunity to teach at a small Christian college. *Was the Lord directing me to marry the professor and have the job of my dreams?* However, my unrest about the relationship plagued me, and so I resisted applying for it.

Time passed and we continued to date, but I knew the day would come when the professor would no longer be patient with me. I felt very conflicted. On one hand I wanted a man in my life and the professor was pretty close to what I wanted. Yet I believed our union would be problematic. I decided to fast for three days in order to hear more clearly from the Lord, but I did not feel as though I got a response. Yet, deep in my heart, I knew the Lord was answering me with "no." I just did not want to acknowledge it. Therefore, I remained in a state of confusion.

The ultimatum finally came that Christmas. "Either we get married, or we will just be friends." My mind swirled. *How could I let him go? He was Christian, smart, attractive, and so very close to what I was seeking.*

I hesitated. "Okay...Let's get married," I feebly replied.

"What would be a good date for you?" he pressed.

"It has to be a time when Anna will be home from college. She has her spring break the first week in March," I offered.

"Okay, let's make it Saturday, March 8," he offered.

"Okay," I agreed reluctantly.

I had finally made the decision, but now I had to tell the kids. Dread filled my heart. I knew they would be upset and put up a fight. I decided to start with Anna, since she was the oldest.

When we were alone driving together, I decided to tell her. I could barely get the words out of my mouth. "The professor and I are getting married in March," I revealed. I was surprised that her response was not as bad as it could have been, but I still felt like throwing up. I never even tried to tell my other three kids.

"I just can't do it," I informed the professor over the phone. It had only been a day since we had made our plans, but I had not been able to sleep the previous night. Instead of feeling joy, I felt as if I were facing a death sentence. I reflected on the fact that I had not experienced this hesitation when I married David.

"Okay, we will be friends, but I am free to look for someone else," he responded. I told him that was fine, glad to at least have some contact with him.

Shortly after we canceled our wedding plans, I received an e-mail from the head of the family and consumer sciences department, asking me to interview for the instructor position. Peter was still recovering from the injuries that he had sustained in an automobile accident, so that was consuming a great deal of my time. My relationship with the professor was in shambles, and, if I got the job, I would have to move to the town where he lived. I e-mailed back, "Thank you so much for considering me, but I have a son that needs my help, so I think I need to pass."

"Oh, just come and at least interview," the department head persisted in her return e-mail. The job had been open for some time now. Not only was there a shortage of family and consumer sciences teachers but, for most candidates, the part-time status hardly justified a move to the small town where the college was located. I found it difficult to decline the request. After all, this was my ideal job, and how many institutions would consider someone with my meager qualifications?

"Okay, I'll come," I agreed.

I spent the three-hour drive to the interview in prayer. Up to this point, I had prayed for my desires—*Send me a man, let me teach.* I knew that if I got the job I would be more tempted to be with the professor. I was in such turmoil now that I vowed to seek the Lord's will instead of what I thought I wanted. "Oh, Lord, I do not know if I'm supposed to have this job. May You be present and guide the proceedings. May Your will ultimately be done."

After arriving at the college and teaching a lesson, I was taken into a room and questioned by a group of professors. The interviewing process went well enough until one of the faculty members offered, "This position is part-time. How do you feel about that?"

I enthusiastically shot back, "I don't mind it at all. In fact, I prefer a part-time position because if anything ever happened to my children . . ." I trailed off. *I could not believe what was happening.* A flood of emotion overtook me, and tears began to well in my eyes and I stopped speaking.

They all paused. "Do you really want the position?" said the interviewer, breaking the silence. *Did I?* All my confidence immediately evaporated. I felt as if I was just a mom—not a college instructor. I grew very quiet and finished the rest of the two-day interview filled with much trepidation.

I had not asked when they would inform me of their decision. Three weeks went by without hearing anything from them. I felt sure they had interviewed me only because of my connection with the professor. It must have been most unappealing to have my mommy emotions spewing all over the place, too.

I was worn out from constantly mulling over my relationship with the professor and having to think about moving. The uncertainty of the job offer was also made me restless. I could not endure the uncertainty any longer. I e-mailed the college: "Thank you so much for considering me for the position of instructor in the family and consumer sciences department. However, I would like to remove my name from consideration." That night was the first night in a long time that I went to sleep without a knot in my stomach and did not toss and turn all night. I felt totally at peace.

The next day I prayed, "Dear Lord, please send a good woman into the professor's life." I felt guilty that I had tied up this man's life for three years and prevented him from finding a woman he could marry. I knew how difficult it was for him bringing up his boys alone. He was a good man and deserved to have someone in his life. The Lord swiftly answered that prayer as five months later, he was married.

I vowed to myself, "I am not going to chase after a man again. If God wants me with someone, He'll bring him to my door." After my relationship with the professor, I was determined to once again concentrate solely upon my children. However, a few years later, the people who lived across the street put their house up for sale and I heard that a man in his fifties was moving into it. He was supposed to be really nice. *A single man . . . across the street . . . was this an answer to my prayer from years ago—was God bringing someone literally to my door?* It seemed odd in this neighborhood of all families that an unmarried man would move in and all of places, directly across from me.

Signs of his impending arrival surfaced. Truckloads of furniture came and went. Then his car started to be parked periodically in the driveway.

One evening my boys were playing in front of our house and they called for me to come out for something. After I dealt with whatever they needed, the man across the street happened to be pulling out from his driveway. We made eye contact, and before I knew it, he leaped out of his car and came running over to me.

"Hi, my name is Mike."

"Hi, I'm Mary."

We continued with small talk awhile as I carefully observed him. He seemed nice and was good-looking enough. Even though I later discovered that this man professed to be a Christian, I was not really interested in getting involved since I observed various women coming and going at his house. Besides, I had not really prayed for a man to enter my life recently, but it did seem odd that this guy would happen to move across the street.

Months passed, and his mere presence constantly reminded me of my own singleness. I was always wondering whether he was home and hated that. "Lord," I pleaded, "Please make him move."

At Christmastime I noticed his car home during the weekdays. Finally, seeing him outside shoveling his driveway, I asked him, "Are you on vacation?"

"No, I lost my job," he confessed.

"Oh, I am so sorry," I said.

Mike had previously been employed with a large company but had always dreamed of managing his own business. When a friend offered him the opportunity to take over his small business, Mike had jumped at the chance. After he transitioned into that job, his companion felt threatened, rethought his decision to retire, and fired him.

Within a couple of months, Mike found another job. He put his house up for sale and relocated to South Carolina. He resided across the street from me for a total of seven months.

Some time passed, and my familiar longings for male companionship once again returned. I determined I really did want a man in my life and reflected upon how many times the Lord had swiftly answered my prayers when I prayed with passion for them. So one night as I lay in bed, armed with this belief, I raised my arms up and cried out loud, "Please send someone into my life."

I felt the answer I received from the Lord was, "I will send someone, but he will not be everything you want."

"Oh, that's okay," I replied. I just wanted someone.

At eight thirty the next morning, my telephone rang. *Who would be calling this early?* I looked at the caller ID and recognized the name as a man that I had met a few years earlier from an online Christian matchmaking site. He was from Florida, slightly older than myself, tall, good-looking, but had had been divorced twice. We had talked for several months back then, but I ended our communications because I began to sense why he may have had issues in his previous marriages. Because of this, I was not anxious to associate with him again, and I could not bring myself to answer the phone.

I had just prayed last night for someone to enter my life, and shockingly, this man was now calling me. *Was this the Lord's answer to my prayer?* However, I understood what He meant when He said the man would not be everything I wanted—I definitely had a few reservations about him. After letting the phone ring through, he left a message. As I listened to it, he shared that his oldest son was getting married in Ann Arbor, Michigan, and he wanted to stop by on his drive up from Florida for the wedding. At the very least, I owed him a return call.

I picked up the phone and dialed his number. He answered and after some small talk, he said, "Can we meet? I was thinking that if everything goes well, I'd like you to be my date for the wedding." This was progress. He had previously insisted that if we were to meet, I would have to be the one to make the trip to Florida. Now he was at least willing to come to my house, even if it was on his way to Michigan.

"All right," I responded, even though I was hesitant.

We renewed our correspondence once again, but it did not take long for my reservations to resurface. I called him and apologized, "I'm sorry. I just don't think we would make a good couple. I hope you can find someone else to go to your son's wedding." He seemed to accept this rejection well enough and we parted our ways once again.

Three times, I offered up prayers encouraging God to send a man into my life. Three times, the Lord answered those prayers. Yet, these occurrences lead to me to analyze how God intervenes into the affairs of man. God has a supreme plan for each person's life and for the world in general. This predestined plan of events is often referred to as God's sovereign will, and will come to pass regardless of any human interference. Proverbs 19:21 confirms this as it outlines, "Many are the plans in a man's heart, but it is the Lord's purpose that prevails."

However, I had witnessed that my prayers had produced results that may not have been what God wanted for me. I sensed that He had other plans that would be more suited for me, yet He seemingly was allowing me to have what I had asked for. I later came to understand that while He has a perfect will for mankind, he gives us the freedom choose our own path as well. It may be, however, that we will not be as happy on our own path as we could be on His.

The ability to deviate from God's perfect wish for us is known as God's permissive will. In Deuteronomy 30:19, we find the challenge, "This day I call heaven and earth as witnesses against you that I have set before you life and death, blessings and curses. Now choose life, so that you and your children may live." God gives us choices. The repercussions of selecting our own path over God's can vary from being very little to having a great impact.[1]

God's permissive will is illustrated several other times in Scripture. In 1 Samuel 8, the elders of the

Israelites wished to have a king appointed over them just as their neighboring nations had. The Lord was displeased with this request and tried to warn them through Samuel of the negative consequences that they would face by having a king. Still, the Israelites refused to relent, so the Lord granted their plea. The Israelites got what they wanted but they ended up suffering under their rulers. They would have been happier if they had followed God's will.

Another example was when King Hezekiah bargained with God after Nathan the prophet approached him and informed him that he was about to die. King Hezekiah pointed out to God that he had led a righteous life and pleaded with God to give him more time. God listened to his petition and granted him fifteen additional years of life.

However, during the fifteen additional years he was given, several negative repercussions came to pass during that time. King Hezekiah was visited by the Babylonians, to whom he showed all his treasures. Later, the Babylonians pillaged the Israelites and confiscated all those riches. Furthermore, King Hezekiah conceived a son during this time who later assumed the throne. This man turned out to be one of the most evil kings that Israel ever had and consequently, led the Israelites far away from God.

Our Lord knows ultimately what is best for us. We are encouraged to make petitions for what we desire, but it seems wise to cover our prayer with "Your will be done." Jesus observed this when he prayed in the Garden of Gethsemane as recorded in Matthew 26:39 where it says, "My Father, if it is possible, may this cup be taken from me. Yet not as I will, but as you will." Jesus understandably was concerned about the difficult circumstances He was about to face, but still wanted God's will over His own. If Jesus had not covered his request in that manner and God realized Jesus' wish, Jesus may have avoided much personal pain. However, if God's will was not followed, then the greater good of forgiveness of sins for mankind would not have been accomplished.

As mere children of God, we are unable to realize all the eventual consequences of our pleas. Usually, we just whine for what we think would satisfy us at the moment. Even if we draw close to the Lord, which will align our desires closer to God's mind, we are still made of flesh and do not possess divine insight.

Therefore, after mulling over these insights, I vowed from then on to make sure that after sending up any pleas to God that His will would ultimately be done. I wanted God's perfect plan for my life because I knew that His path would bring me the greatest happiness—with or without a man.

Scripture

Proverbs 19:2-3: "It is not good to have zeal without knowledge, nor to be hasty and miss the way. A man's own folly ruins his life, yet his heart rages against the LORD."

Matthew 6:10: Your kingdom come, your will be done on earth as it is in heaven

Example of the Lord's plan being changed

Genesis 19:17-21:

As soon as they had brought them out, one of them said, "Flee for your lives! Don't look back, and don't stop anywhere in the plain! Flee to the mountains or you will be swept away!" But Lot said to them, "No, my lords, please! Your servant has found favor in your eyes, and you have shown great kindness to me in sparing my life. But I can't flee to the mountains; this disaster will overtake me, and I'll die. Look, here is a town near enough to run to, and it is small. Let me flee to it—it is very small, isn't it? Then my life will be spared." He said to him, "Very well, I will grant this request too; I will not overthrow the town you speak of.

1 Samuel 8:4-21:

So all the elders of Israel gathered together and came to Samuel at Ramah. They said to him, "You are old, and your sons do not walk in your ways; now appoint a king to lead us, such as all the other nations have."

But when they said, "Give us a king to lead us," this displeased Samuel; so he prayed to the LORD. And the LORD told him: "Listen to all that the people are saying to you; it is not you they have rejected, but they have rejected me as their king. As they have done from the day I brought them up out of Egypt until this day, forsaking me and serving other gods, so they are doing to you. Now listen to them;

but warn them solemnly and let them know what the king who will reign over them will do."

Samuel told all the words of the LORD to the people who were asking him for a king. He said, "This is what the king who will reign over you will do: He will take your sons and make them serve with his chariots and horses, and they will run in front of his chariots. Some he will assign to be commanders of thousands and commanders of fifties, and others to plow his ground and reap his harvest, and still others to make weapons of war and equipment for his chariots. He will take your daughters to be perfumers and cooks and bakers. He will take the best of your fields and vineyards and olive groves and give them to his attendants. He will take a tenth of your grain and of your vintage and give it to his officials and attendants. Your menservants and maidservants and the best of your cattle and donkeys he will take for his own use. He will take a tenth of your flocks, and you yourselves will become his slaves. When that day comes, you will cry out for relief from the king you have chosen, and the LORD will not answer you in that day."

But the people refused to listen to Samuel. "No!" they said. "We want a king over us. Then we will be like all the other nations, with a king to lead us and to go out before us and fight our battles."

When Samuel heard all that the people said, he repeated it before the LORD.

2 Kings 20:1-6:

In those days Hezekiah became ill and was at the point of death. The prophet Isaiah son of Amoz went to him and said, "This is what the LORD says: Put your house in order, because you are going to die; you will not recover."

Hezekiah turned his face to the wall and prayed to the LORD, "Remember, O LORD, how I have walked before you faithfully and with wholehearted devotion and have done what is good in your eyes." And Hezekiah wept bitterly.

Before Isaiah had left the middle court, the word of the LORD came to him: "Go back and tell Hezekiah, the leader of my people, 'This is what the LORD, the God of your father David, says: I have heard your prayer and seen your tears; I will heal you. On the third day from now you will go up to the temple of the LORD. I will add fifteen years to your life. And I will deliver you and this city from the hand of the king of Assyria. I will defend this city for my sake and for the sake of my servant David.'"

—25—

How the Holy Spirit
Guides Us: Two

A fter David had been gone for four years, I began to think about getting a job. Even though the Lord had provided for me to stay home with my four children so far, I realized that eventually I would need to find work. I believed substituting would help ease my introduction back into the teaching field, so I filled out all the necessary papers and submitted them. Then, on the night of my son Peter's open house at the intermediate high school, I decided to stop by the family and consumer sciences department to introduce myself.

"Hi, my name is Mary. I just signed up to be a substitute in the district. I have my degree in family and consumer sciences education, so if you ever need someone to cover your classes, please give me a call."

Mrs. Packard was the only family and consumer science teacher present. She replied, "Hi. It is nice to meet you. Both of the other FCS teachers have left already, but one of them is having some health issues and is scheduled to have surgery in December. We actually are looking for a long-term substitute, beginning in mid-December. Let me take your name and telephone number and we will get back with you."

I received a call about the position not long afterwards. After meeting with the teacher who wanted the leave of absence, I was offered the job and accepted it. The experience went well, and I even did another long term substitution the next year for the same teacher. After that, a permanent position opened up, which the teachers encouraged me to pursue. It amazed me to be considered for this opportunity because I was getting older, but, then again, they had little choice as there were so very few people who had family and consumer sciences degrees.

I prayed about it, but did not have a peace about pursuing it. Instead, I chose to continue to substitute on a daily basis, which would give me more flexibility to be available for my children. In the back of my mind, I kept reflecting on the rumors that I heard that Margaret, a family and consumer sciences teacher in the middle school, was going to retire in a few years. I reasoned that I could hold out for her position so that my children would be a little older before I gained full-time employment.

The year before Margaret was going to retire, she announced that she needed a long-term substitute for several months. She wanted to undergo a knee replacement before she lost her present health insurance and asked me if I was interested filling the position. Once again I prayed, but I felt the Holy Spirit strongly tell me not pursue it. Nevertheless, I argued with God that they wouldn't have a qualified family and consumer sciences teacher if I didn't take it. Everyone would be depending upon me since I often substituted for them. Besides, if I refused this job, they would be less likely to offer me the permanent position when it became available the following year. After justifying it in my own mind, I decided to take the job.

"I'd be happy to take the position," I informed Margaret.

"That's great! You're already familiar with my classes," Margaret replied.

Adjusting to the new schedule this job required was difficult for me. Getting up at five in the morning, dealing with the demands of teaching full-time, and tending to my four children were draining my energy. By the end of the third school day, I was totally exhausted. I had always required an abundance of sleep and my body pleaded with me to just go home, make dinner quickly, and head to bed. I chastised myself for my weakness, and after dinner that evening, I decided to push myself to at least preview some of the class videos that I had brought home with me.

The television with the VCR was located in our basement. I made my way down there and settled on the couch to view the tapes. After watching several, I put in the last one about money management, which was recorded from an episode of from *The Oprah Show*. It divulged how some people had saved money in a variety of ways and had become millionaires.

When this part ended, another piece began that was of a spiritual nature. "Everything happens to you for a reason," the clip shared. My mind quickly reflected on all the trials I had faced in recent years, and I thought to myself, Yeah, yeah. I know. Unfortunately, I did not realize that those words were not referring to the past events in my life, but to what was about to happen. I then turned off the TV to go upstairs since only the financial segment was important for the course. I got up, gathered the videos together, turned off the VCR, and switched off the overhead light.

Although the room was rather dim without the light on, a fluorescent light from around the corner at gave off some illumination. Having lived here for fifteen years, I had often navigated my way to the stairs in this same lighting many times without incident. However, this time it was different.

As I began my trek across the room, I suddenly felt as though total darkness overtook me. Maybe it was just my tiredness catching up with me but, whatever the cause, a veil seemed to enshroud my eyes. Then, I felt my foot catch upon something and I began to fall. My mind raced frantically—*what in the world am I tripping over?*

I forcibly struck the carpeted basement floor and excruciating pain immediately emanated from my left foot. I must have screamed, because my youngest son, Paul, came running from upstairs. He shot off a myriad of questions, but I had difficulty responding. I felt like I was having an out of the body experience from the intense pain, but gradually I regained some sense of my being.

I was curious what was responsible for my fall. I looked down at my foot and observed that my foot was caught between the legs of a folding chair that I had purchased a few days prior. I had earlier directed one of my children to take it to the basement, but swore I had previously seen it in the corner of the room.

"I must have broken my foot," I told Paul.

"Do you want to go to the emergency room?" Paul asked with concern.

It sounded like the practical thing to do, but I was still exhausted. I pictured it taking hours to have a doctor look at my foot, so I replied, "No, I'm just going to crawl up to my bedroom. Please just get me a bag of ice. I'll deal with it tomorrow."

As my foot was still throbbing the next morning, Peter, who was home on break from college, drove me to the emergency room. After a doctor examined my foot, he informed me, "You really did a good job. You have broken quite a few bones in your foot. I'm going to wrap it in a temporary cast. However, you will need to see an orthopedic doctor to get a permanent one."

I went home and scheduled an appointment for two days later. After the specialist appraised the x-rays and my foot, he directed, "We are going to put a regular cast on your foot, which you will need to wear for about six weeks."

"I just began a long-term substituting job. Do you think I can go back to work?" I asked.

"Do you absolutely have to? If you do, then you can go. However, if you do go back, you will be in tears by the end of the day," he shared.

I thought it over in my mind. If I had been very worn out after the school day when my foot was fine, I knew I would not be able to handle each day in a cast. Besides, it was the beginning of January and was going to be icy outside, so I opted to leave the position.

Once I was home, I reflected how this mishap answered a recent prayer of mine that my sons would become more self-sufficient. Now, since I had a broken foot and couldn't to do much work around the house, this prayer was soon realized. Using crutches made cleaning, meal preparation, and other household tasks quite laborious, so I transferred as many chores as possible to my boys. If I had not broken my foot, I would have been tempted to just do the work myself, even though I wanted my boys to learn these responsibilities. Now, however, they were forced to become more independent.

This accident also enabled me to discover a way I could teach and still be home with my children. Confined to mostly sitting, I transferred my energies into constructing an online course. This new avenue of teaching was becoming quite popular, and I had been interested in exploring this as a possibility for some time. Periodically, I searched the Internet for classes that taught how to construct courses for online schools, but I never was successful in finding one. Then that past fall, I happen to discover a course-building software company that was offering a free trial and was tempted to develop a college-level class on parenting. However, all of my housework and my children's needs distracted me, so I never got very far. Now, since I wasn't capable of doing much of anything else, I was able to work on it frequently.

I finished building this online course in the spring of that year, but I didn't have an opportunity for utilizing it. Instead, the middle school family and consumer sciences teacher position was now officially advertised, so I prayed once again about whether I should pursue it. This was a permanent position that would afford me a steady income and health benefits. Additionally, it was in the human development area, which was my favorite subject in my field. Being in my children's school district would also mean I would be on my children's schedule, which would be another bonus. I reasoned to myself that this would to be my final chance to secure a teaching job at our school since no other positions appeared to upcoming in the near future. Anyway, the district probably was getting frustrated with my refusal to pursue previous openings. Yet, that fear of not being there for my children loomed.

I prayed and said to myself, "I'll read my Bible and see if anything pops out at me." I had heard that someone had nicknamed this practice as "Bible roulette," and that one should avoid trying it. On the other hand, I remember a missionary visiting to our church and sharing a story with me. He had decided to read his Bible to console himself when the girl of his dreams was walking out of his life. One particular verse popped out, which conveyed to him that she would later become his wife. A year later, they got married. Thinking about this, I figured I'd see what I came up with anyway.

I began to read a few passages, but they shed little insight into my situation. Maybe this was foolishness. Then, I turned to 2 John 1. It began with, "To the chosen lady and her children." That certainly sparked my interest. Although I did not believe I was "chosen," the idea that it was speaking to just a woman, without a husband, and her children intrigued me. In all the times I read the Bible through, I never recalled anything being directed solely to my particular situation. I read on. "Some of your children are walking with the Lord." I mulled that over and concluded that it also could apply to my family. "Watch out that you do not lose what you have worked for, but that you may be rewarded fully."

Wow. I knew this passage could be taken many different ways, but since David's death, I had made it my primary mission to stay at home and be a consistent figure for my children. I believed they would fare much better if they had one parent who had sufficient energy for all the issues they would face in their lives and who would not be preoccupied with work. The Lord had been gracious and had provided for my family enough so that I didn't have to work full-time.

I decided to take this Scripture as telling me not to pursue this job. I didn't want all the previous time I had invested raising my kids to become meaningless if my children would suffer. I needed to continue in the path I had started.

It was not easy to do what I believed the Lord was telling me to do. It required me to have faith that the Lord would continue to meet our family's financial needs. Currently, I felt secure, but if I looked down the road, I could rationalize that I should be doing more to ensure financial security. I chose to trust the Lord, as He had not failed me in the past. I also didn't want any repercussions from being disobedient.

I continued to substitute instead. Then, about a year later, my next-door neighbor Patti, encouraged me to send my résumé to a cyber high school where she had become a Spanish teacher the year before. Although I had originally pictured myself teaching at the college level, I submitted my résumé anyway. I was called in for an interview, and brought with me the online course I had developed earlier. They seemed impressed and offered me the opportunity to develop and teach a comprehensive course in family and consumer sciences for grades nine through twelve.

Although I had originally been hesitant about taking this online position, I soon discovered it was a perfect match for me. I immensely enjoyed the daily lesson preparation and the creativity this style of teaching afforded. I also appreciated the flexibility it afforded me to be there for my children.

Two years after that, I proposed the possibility to the school principal to teach a parenting class, which was a subject near and dear to my heart. He approved of the idea, so, I was able to teach the two of my favorite subjects in a way that worked perfectly for me.

The Holy Spirit had led me through a variety of circumstances to find a position that met both my needs and those of my children. A long-term substituting position just happened to be opening up that introduced me back to the teaching field. When I tried to take on a position that I wasn't supposed to take, I broke my foot, which prevented me from continuing. While recuperating, I had time to learn how to teach online using a program I just happened to discover a few months earlier. A Bible verse prevented me from seeking a full-time position. My next door neighbor opened the door for me to teach at a cyber school. God seemed to guide me in getting a job that suited me best.

Scripture

God fashioning circumstances in Joseph's life

Genesis 37:28: So when the Midianite merchants came by, his brothers pulled Joseph up out of the cistern and sold him for twenty shekels of silver to the Ishmaelites, who took him to Egypt.

Genesis 39:2: The LORD was with Joseph so that he prospered, and he lived in the house of his Egyptian master.

Genesis 39:20-22: Joseph's master took him and put him in prison, the place where the king's prisoners were confined. But while Joseph was there in the prison, the LORD was with him; he showed him kindness and granted him favor in the eyes of the prison warden. So the warden put Joseph in charge of all those held in the prison, and he was made responsible for all that was done there.

Genesis 41:8: In the morning his mind was troubled, so he sent for all the magicians and wise men of Egypt. Pharaoh told them his dreams, but no one could interpret them for him.

Genesis 41:12: Now a young Hebrew was there with us, a servant of the captain of the guard. We told him our dreams, and he interpreted them for us, giving each man the interpretation of his dream.

Genesis 41:39-40: Then Pharaoh said to Joseph, "Since God has made all this known to you, there is no one so discerning and wise as you. You shall be in charge of my palace, and all my people are to submit to your orders. Only with respect to the throne will I be greater than you.

Trusting God

"Guess what, Mom?" Peter, my oldest son, asked excitedly. "I have an internship with an engineering company in Austin, Texas for the summer!" A junior at Virginia Tech, Peter was majoring in computer engineering and had been exploring various opportunities to gain some experience in his field. "That's great, Peter!" I exclaimed. I asked about his position a little, and then I was curious where he would stay for the summer. "Is housing provided for the interns, or will you have to find somewhere to live?"

"We have to find our own place, but they gave us a list of apartment complexes and the name of a real estate person to contact. The offer letter also listed the names of a few people looking for a roommate. There's one guy who seems like he would be okay," Peter told me.

As we talked, I reflected that this would be Peter's first major step into the real world, and he might not find many Christians in the business world. The person he lived with could also have a major impact upon his faith, so I prayed that Peter would find a Christian with whom to live. That way, if he faced ridicule or pressure to get involved in any immoral activities, he would have some Christian support.A few weeks later, Peter shared with me that he had contacted the boy who placed the ad in the company letter, but he had already found a roommate. He continued, "I talked with the real estate guy they recommended, and he has the names of a couple of places with three-month leases and said I should move quickly. Also, a guy e-mailed all the people in our particular assignment area and asked if anyone would like to get an apartment with him," Peter said. "He said he goes to Penn State and says the school's colors blue and white runs through his veins. He sounds like a fun guy, even if he does like to party. I think I'll write back and see if I can room with him."

A few days later, Alberto, the guy who e-mailed everyone, wrote back to Peter. He told him that someone else had contacted him first but that all three of them could room together. Peter said that it was fine with him and that he had already been in contact with a real estate agent about finding an apartment. He would now tell the realtor to look for a three-bedroom unit for all of them.

When Peter shared this latest development with me, I was not thrilled. Alberto did not sound like he was an answer to my prayer, so I was not happy.

A few weeks later, the company sent out a personality profile for all the interns to complete in an effort for the interns to find roommates that would be compatible. When Peter disclosed this to me, I urged Peter, "Are you sure you want to room with him? Maybe you should use that personality profile to find someone better suited to you." I was hoping to divert Peter from the rooming with this partier, thinking he might be a bad influence on Peter. I thought using this diagnostic device would hopefully connect Peter with someone more in line with his conservative outlook on life.

"No, I'm just going to stay with Alberto," Peter answered, much to my disappointment. I decided not to say anything more, and Peter went ahead with the plans to get the apartment with Alberto and the other person who had responded to Alberto's email. I was upset that the situation did not work out as I expected.

When summer came, Peter settled into his apartment in Texas and started his internship. A week or two later, he called to tell me how everything was going.

"Hey, Mom, you know the other guy that Alberto had lined up as a roommate before me? Well, he is a really dedicated Christian. He prays all the time with such depth and was involved with Campus Crusade for Christ at his school. He even did witnessing on street corners back in his hometown. He puts my Christian walk to shame," Peter confessed. I was elated! God had answered my prayer in a way I never expected.

That roommate ended up strengthening Peter's faith significantly, and he grew spiritually by leaps and bounds during that summer. This roommate and Peter even influenced Alberto to start going to church.

Even though I prayed over it, I had almost messed up everything by encouraging Peter to not choose Alberto. I really should have just trusted God as he provided the perfect roommates for Peter.

Scripture

Proverbs 3:5: Trust in the LORD with all your heart and lean not on your own understanding.

Isaiah 26:4: Trust in the LORD forever, for the LORD, the LORD himself, is the Rock eternal.

James 1: 6-7: But when he asks, he must believe and not doubt, because he who doubts is like a wave of the sea, blown and tossed by the wind. That man should not think he will receive anything from the Lord; he is a double-minded, unstable in all he does.

— 27 —

Healing

In Mark 16:15-18, Jesus commissions believers to "Go into all the world and preach the good news to all creation. Whoever believes and is baptized will be saved, but whoever does not believe will be condemned. And these signs will accompany those who believe: In my name they will drive out demons; they will speak in new tongues; they will pick up snakes with their bare hands; and when they drink deadly poison, it will not hurt them at all; they will place their hands on sick people, and they will get well."

I had often heard this verse recited as an instruction to witness to others, but the subsequent abilities that a believer is supposed to possess puzzled me. Although I had witnessed people speaking in tongues, I never had seen anyone drive out a demon, pick up snakes with their bare hands, drink deadly poison and live, or lay hands upon a sick person and have them be healed. Yet, here in Scripture, it stated that those who believe in Jesus seemingly should be capable of achieving such feats.

The discrepancy between the truth stated in the Scripture and my personal experience never really plagued me though. I just chalked it up to one of those confusing things in the Bible that I would never be privileged enough to understand. However, God eventually guided me in exploring one of these promised signs, which was the gift of healing.

I first became interested in healing when I read a book about it, which I only discovered by chance. A secretary at the cyber school where I was teaching had it on the table in front of her while she was monitoring teachers voting about unionizing. Noticing from the cover that it might have a Christian theme, I asked, "What's that book you are reading?"

"*Greater Works* by Smith Wigglesworth," she replied. She handed it to me to peruse. It looked interesting, so I jotted down the name. A few weeks later, I purchased it at my local Christian bookstore.

I found that it was a compilation of sermons written by an eighteenth century preacher about ways to draw upon the Holy Spirit to heal others. The preface revealed that the author had cured many people of illnesses in his lifetime. Yet, some had complained that he handled people roughly and yelled viciously at them. He defended himself by saying that he was angry at the devil, the source of their sickness.

Even though many were healed around him, his own family faced afflictions. His wife and son died before him, his daughter was deaf for her entire life, and he battled with kidney stones and sciatica.[1] However, his numerous accounts of healing others stirred my curiosity about whether this gift was available for today and people just weren't attempting to utilize it.

During the time that I was reading this book, I also happened to see the tail end of a documentary about healing called *The Finger of God*. Although I rarely watched TV, for some reason I had turned the TV and this broadcast piqued my interest, so I sent away for a copy of the DVD. When it arrived, I was finally able to watch the entire film.

The man who created the DVD embarked on this project because his own aunt and uncle seemingly had gold teeth appear in their mouths as an answer to prayer. The filmmaker knew his own family was trustworthy and wondered how often healings like that were happening today. So, he went around the world citing specific incidents of miraculous healings for his movie. [2] Hearing about all the healings in the movie made me even more interested to learn about this mysterious gift.

About a month after viewing that video, I flew to Austin, where I was planning to stay a month to visit my son and his wife. I wanted to test out if I would like living in that area sometime in the future. I stayed at the house of a woman who advertised on Craigslist about renting out one of her bedrooms on a short-term basis. On my first full day there, I met this woman's cousin, who was visiting her from out of town. He was a man about my age and we all somehow got into a conversation about healing. He revealed that he was capable of curing others and that he actually had brought someone back from the dead. He talked about it a little, and I was amazed that the topic of healing was coming up so much in my life recently.

Additionally, during my time in Austin, I expressed interest to my son's in-laws about visiting the church where they regularly attended. The church was known to draw upon the gifts of the Spirit and I was curious about it. When I asked about going with them to the next Sunday's service, they also encouraged me to go to a three-day conference their church was having that week. Although I didn't recognize the name of the featured speaker, I decided to attend because they seemed excited about it.

When I went, I discovered that the speaker, Bill Johnson, was a pastor from California who ran an institute that focused on healing. He shared some of the many success stories that he and his students had the privilege of witnessing. At the end of each night, he had us pray for each other. Then those who claimed to have received an immediate healing would come up and share what ailment they previously had.

On the third night, it dawned on me that this speaker was actually one of the men that had been interviewed on the *Finger of God* DVD that I had recently purchased. All these "coincidental" exposures of people being healed amazed me. It seemed like they were coming into my life one right after another.

After returning home from Austin, I discussed these occurrences with one of my Christian girlfriends. She recently had switched churches and informed me that her new church was holding a ten-week class about healing. Since the Lord seemed to keep having this topic present itself to me, I was eager to have some guidance on this topic and signed up for it.

My first impression of this church class was that it was a little cult-like. During the first session, we were informed that no one could ask questions and that only positive comments would be tolerated. They tried to convince us that all our questions would be eventually be answered. I also learned that a new policy was going to soon prevent non-members of the church from taking the class. This seemed to be in conflict with the more frequent desire of churches to draw in as many people as possible. This made me very wary, but, since this was the only church I knew of that even dealt with trying to heal, I chose to continue to attend.

The strongest argument presented in the course was that when Jesus was on earth, He never failed to heal someone when they approached Him. He never said, "No, I think this infirmity will teach you a lesson."

The primary Scripture verse that they used to support their idea that we have the ability to heal was Isaiah 53:4-5 that says, "Surely he took up our infirmities and carried our sorrows, yet we considered him punished by God, stricken by him, and afflicted. But he was pierced for our transgressions, he was crushed for our iniquities; the punishment that brought us peace was on him, and by his wounds we are healed." They claimed that both our sins and our diseases were removed at the cross. If we only turned to the Lord, He would give us grace to conquer them.

Reflecting on this verse, though, I believed that this restoration would be finished in the future since we continue to struggle with not only disease but also sin. Romans 8:23 seems to confirm this since it says, "But we ourselves, who have the firstfruits of the Spirit, groan inwardly as we wait eagerly for our adoption as sons, the redemption of our bodies."

We were also instructed that healings fail to take place is because our hearts aren't persuaded. We had to have faith, and faith comes from reading the Bible and believing in the verses that support healing for today.

Therefore, we couldn't be in the presence of people who doubted, they said, which meant we should isolate ourselves from people who were skeptical. According to them, only then should we begin to pray for healing.

They stated that it would only be necessary to pray once because if we continued to beseech the Lord about the matter, that would mean we didn't believe in the healing the first time we prayed. They supported this idea with the story of Lazarus being brought back from the dead. In the story, Jesus thanked God for bringing Lazarus back to life before he had even immerged from the tomb. Therefore, they said after praying, we should believe that the healing has immediately taken place and thank the Lord, even if no signs of restoration are apparent.

I was not sure of this church's described method of healing. Both Luke 11:5-8 and Luke 18:1-8 encourage believers to be persistent in praying, however, this group instructed us to only pray once. Also, saying someone was healed without actually seeing evidence of healing could be potentially dangerous. The Lord may allow someone to face an illness or health issue for whatever purpose according to His will. So, if a person does not receive a healing, they or others may find discouragement if they believe this church's ideas about healing.

Additionally, they believed that God created us to be happy. They told us to picture Him as a parent. The leader asked, "Which of you parents doesn't want your children to have good health, be wealthy, and have satisfaction in life?" He continued that the reason we don't currently possess these things is that we haven't drawn upon God's grace to obtain them. I felt that this view was wrong. I believed the Lord allowed trials into our life to discipline us and shape us more closely into His image. Although I did not wish harm upon my children, the thought of a strictly easy life for my children might make them self-centered and complacent.

Right after the class where we were told that God wanted us to be happy, I left to attend my own church's service, which was later that morning. When I arrived, I discovered that my pastor happened to be out of town. Instead of hearing him preach, we viewed a video presentation given by Craig Groeschel, a minister who our pastor respected. As the presentation started, I felt the preacher in the video was looking directly at me when he said, "God wants you to be happy. God has good things in store for you. God wants you to enjoy your life. God wants you to prosper in every single way."

Since I trusted most things my church promoted and this preacher was agreeing with what I had just questioned from the healing class, it wondered if my thoughts were incorrect. Then, the minister quickly changed gears and offered arguments against this type of thinking. He shared when we think this way, we are reducing the God of the universe to being our servant. We begin to worship the false god of comfort. Happiness is based only on the things of this world—possessions, relationships, appearances, and peaceful circumstances, which contradicts 1 John 2:15, which states, "Do not love the world or anything in the world. If anyone loves the world, love for the Father is not in them."[3] I then felt relieved as his comments verified some of the discomfort I was feeling about the ideas being taught in the healing class.

Even though it make me question the validity of the information in this class even more, I still attended because I was curious to know what further arguments they had. It also was difficult to dismiss everything they said because occasionally they have some good points. It made me wonder at times if there were some grounds for some of their ideas.

During the time period when I was taking this class, I had an experience where I felt moved to pray for someone to have a physical restoration. It was summer at the time and our church was having church gathering in our local park to celebrate the past week of doing acts of service for our community. I had attended this special service the previous year and prayed ahead of time that God would let me sit with someone as I had gone alone. He rewarded that prayer as a couple had come over to me and asked if they could sit with me. We ended up having a very nice conversation, so this gave me confidence to try again this year, so I again prayed for some company this year.

As I walked over to the grassy space in front of the amphitheater where this event was taking place, I glanced around me. I didn't see anyone that I knew and this disheartened me. I placed my folding chair in an area that was slightly off-center from the stage and then made my way over to where the food was being served. I still didn't see anyone that I knew. I only had been going to this church for about a year, but the previous Sunday, I finally felt like I was making connections with people. Yet, here I was again feeling rather isolated.

Painfully aware of my singleness, I took my food and went back to my seat to eat. After finishing up the meal, I noted that there was still about twenty-five minutes before the service was to begin. Sporadically, a few people I knew passed by me and said hi, but made no offer to either sit with me or have me join them. When the service began I thought, *"Well, God you really didn't answer my prayer this year,"* and I wondered why.

As the worship team began, I joined in singing, but I was not happy at all. After a couple of songs, our pastor instructed us to greet those around us and share with them what project we had done during the past week.

I turned around to find an older couple sitting behind me. The man introduced himself and his wife and started to say something else to me when a girlfriend of mine excitedly came up and unknowingly cut the man off. She showed me some pictures of the food bank shelves that were empty and then pictures of them full after she and others had collected food that afternoon. I felt bad that this man had been interrupted, but I politely listened. When we finished conversing, she went back to her seat, and since the church had already resumed singing songs, I just returned to mine.

It bothered me that I hadn't finished talking to the man behind me. I kept thinking that I should turn around and apologize and ask him what else he wanted to tell me. Finally, a break came from the songs, and I turned around and said, "I'm sorry. We got cut off. What else did you want to tell me?"

"I just was going to say that my wife and I had been out of town and were busy so we didn't do a project this week," he replied.

"I didn't do one either this week. Mine is actually coming up next week," I confessed.

This man went on to share that his wife had been a kindergarten teacher, but now she suffered with tremors in her one hand. Since the Lord had kept exposing me to the idea of praying for others for healing, the thought immediately came to me to ask this woman if she would mind me praying for her shaking hand. I believed she might think I was completely nuts for doing so, but when I asked, she shocked me as she seemed completely open to accepting my offer. I grasped her hand in both of mine and prayed, "Lord, I ask for complete healing from these tremors. I feel You have asked me to pray for this woman. Please heal her in Jesus' name, Amen." I felt my prayer was so simple and so inadequate, but happy that I had at least ventured an attempt to have God address her health issue.

Right after asking this request, the woman's husband started shuffling about and directed me, "Sit in my seat and I'm going to sit in yours." As he said that, I felt that this woman had something to share with me and I was right.

This woman, whose name was Pam, began to say, "About a year ago, I went shopping with my mother and two daughters. After we got out of the car and walked up to the shops, two men approached me and said, "We see you are having trouble walking. What is wrong'"

"I've been having lots of problems with my hip," she informed them. She told me that she was amazed because she hadn't known that her problem was that visible.

"We would like to pray for you," they shared.

"All right," she agreed and so they did.

Pam then went on to say that she was not immediately healed, but that it took about two or three days. She continued to say that she hadn't experienced any more problems with her hip to this day. This made me understand why this couple had responded to my request so willingly. They probably felt maybe my gesture was God-ordained and that she would again receive a healing. Her account also comforted me, as I noticed that my prayer for her had not stopped her hand from quivering.

I never found out if my prayers were answered for this woman. However, her story had given me hope that I had indeed heard from God to pray for her. I also noted that my original prayer of sitting with others had been fulfilled.

This encounter encouraged me that healing is a gift for today, and I continued to have materials related to this subject come across my path. One such item was a video clip sent to me through email about a healing that had occurred in 2006. It was a reenactment of a man going to the emergency room with chest pains. He ended up suffering a heart attack when he arrived in the waiting room. Doctors desperately worked upon him for about forty minutes. During this time, the cardiologist on duty, Dr. Chauncey Crandall, was called in to examine him. Seeing no signs of life, he pronounced the man to be dead. However, as Dr. Crandall was leaving the examining room, he felt a voice telling him to go back and pray for this man. He bucked that feeling, but then thought he heard it again. Fearing he would be disobedient, he decided to act upon the prodding. He turned around and went back to the area where the heart attack victim was now being prepared for the morgue by a nurse.

When Dr. Crandall explained to the nurse what he wanted to do, she looked at him in disbelief, but she stopped what she was doing. Dr. Crandall prayed over the man and then the thought came to him that he should use the paddles on him. He then directed another doctor, who had now come back into the room, to try the paddles again. The other doctor argued with him. He said that they already had tried them a dozen times. However, out of respect for Dr. Crandall, this doctor carried out the request. Immediately after shocking the man's chest, he was revived. First he began to breathe and then his fingers and arms started to move. Dr. Crandall shared that the man's heartbeat was instantly normal, which never occurs in such situations. The patient was then taken to intensive care and, by three days, he was sitting up in bed and was doing well.

After the portrayal of the event, Pat Robertson, the host of the television show *The 700 Club*, interviewed Dr. Crandall. Dr. Crandall confessed that he was not feeling particularly spiritual that day. He just followed the prompting that he felt. He claimed that we only need the amount of faith the size of a mustard seed for God to intervene.

Mr. Robertson's questioning went on to reveal that Dr. Crandall had a son that was diagnosed with leukemia six years prior to this event. That diagnosis had inspired Dr. Crandall to immerse himself in Scripture, as he ended up reading the entire Bible three times in that year.[4]

This event got me thinking that we possibly are supposed to listen for God's direction before attempting to heal others. I then happened upon the book, *Spiritual Authority* by Watchman Nee, which supported the idea that our actions should be initiated by God. It quoted Matthew 7:21-23 that reads, "Not everyone who says to me, 'Lord, Lord,' will enter the kingdom of heaven, but only the one who does the will of my Father who is in heaven. Many will say to me on that day, 'Lord, Lord, did we not prophesy in your name and in your name drive out demons and in your name perform many miracles?' Then I will tell them plainly, 'I never knew you. Away from me, you evildoers!'" He ascertained that people who did these supernatural acts were scolded because they made themselves as their starting point instead of being guided by the Lord.[5]

The mere fact that a healing took place does not mean it comes from God. Satan tries to mimic everything in God's realm. When Moses performed miracles, Pharaoh's evil sorcerers and the magicians were also able to accomplish the same things. To me, this indicates that unless healings are directed by the Lord, they may be originating from wicked sources, and thus, would be displeasing to God.

God always wants us to look to Him for guidance about what acts to do for Him, so it would make sense that He would direct us when to heal others as well. Even though Mark 16 commands us to heal others as Peter did in Acts, we need to be attentive to God's prompting before proceeding.

This doesn't mean that we can't petition the Lord for healings to occur. In fact, the most direct passage in Scripture about healing is James 5:14-15, which instructs the afflicted to go to the elders of the church and have them pray over them and anoint them with oil in the name of the Lord. James 5:16 tells us to "Confess your sins to each other and pray for each other so that you may be healed." Philippians 4:6 directs us to pray about all things. Additionally, in contrast to what I was taught in the healing class, you should be persistent in presenting these petitions to God as illustrated in Luke 11:5-8 and Luke 18:1-8.

I do not claim to know all the mysteries surrounding healing. However, I can make a few conclusions from my studying of the topic and my experiences. Firstly, in Dr. Crandall's case, he immersed himself in Scripture prior to being instructed to heal this man, so maybe this exposure to God's Word makes it more conducive for Him to use us for healing others. Secondly, we should be attentive to God's leading concerning healing so that we are doing His will. Finally, we should pray for others who are ill and have them anointed by the elders of the church. Then we can look to the Lord to act and restore health to us and those around us. However, if it does not happen, we must accept that God is sovereign and for whatever reason, He is not allowing the healing to occur.

Scripture

Mark 16:15-18 (Italics added): He said to them, "Go into all the world and preach the good news to all creation. Whoever believes and is baptized will be saved, but whoever does not believe will be condemned. And these signs will accompany those who believe: In my name they will drive out demons; they will speak in new tongues; they will pick up snakes with their hands; and when they drink deadly poison, it will not hurt them at all; they will *place their hands on sick people*, and they will get well."

1 Corinthians 12:9: To another faith by the same Spirit, to another gifts of healing by that one Spirit.

1 Corinthians 12:28: And in the church God has appointed first of all apostles, second prophets, third teachers, then workers of miracles, also those having gifts of healing, of helping, those able to help others, those with gifts of administration, and those speaking in different kinds of tongues.

Matthew 7:21-23: "Not everyone who says to me, 'Lord, Lord,' will enter the kingdom of heaven, but only he who does the will of my Father who is in heaven. Many will say to me on that day, 'Lord, Lord, did we not prophesy in your name, and in your name drive out demons and perform many miracles?' Then I will tell them plainly, 'I never knew you. Away from me, you evildoers!'"

Philippians 4:6: Do not be anxious about anything, but in everything, by prayer and petition, with thanksgiving, present your requests to God.

James 5:14-15: Is any one of you sick? He should call the elders of the church to pray over him and anoint him with oil in the name of the Lord. And the prayer offered in faith will make the sick person well; the Lord will raise him up. If he has sinned, he will be forgiven.

James 5:16: Therefore confess your sins to each other and pray for each other so that you may be healed.

Luke 11:5-8:

> Then he said to them, "Suppose one of you has a friend, and he goes to him at midnight and says, 'Friend, lend me three loaves of bread, because a friend of mine on a journey has come to me, and I have nothing to set before him.'
> "Then the one inside answers, 'Don't bother me. The door is already locked, and my children are with

me in bed. I can't get up and give you anything.' I tell you, though he will not get up and give him the bread because he is his friend, yet because of the man's boldness he will get up and give him as much as he needs.

Luke 18:1-8:

Then Jesus told his disciples a parable to show them that they should always pray and not give up. He said: "In a certain town there was a judge who neither feared God nor cared about men. And there was a widow in that town who kept coming to him with the plea, 'Grant me justice against my adversary.'"For some time he refused. But finally he said to himself, 'Even though I don't fear God or care about men, yet because this widow keeps bothering me, I will see that she gets justice, so that she won't eventually wear me out with her coming!'"And the Lord said, "Listen to what the unjust judge says. And will not God bring about justice for his chosen ones, who cry out to him day and night? Will he keep putting them off? I tell you, he will see that they get justice, and quickly. However, when the Son of Man comes, will he find faith on the earth?"

—28—

Acting on Faith

A t the beginning of one summer, I was looking for some spiritually-based book to read or a Bible study to complete. I happened to find the workbook associated with the book *Experiencing God*. It looked interesting to me, and it was broken up into daily sections. I thought it might be a good project to complete over the upcoming weeks of when I would have more free time.

From these lessons, I learned the principle that God approaches mankind with tasks that He desires each person to accomplish.[1] There are many references to this in Scripture to support this. For example, Abraham was told to move to a new land and that he would father a son and have many descendants. Noah was instructed to build an ark. Saul and David were each advised that they would become a king. Jonah was instructed to go to Nineveh to preach against the behavior of the people of that town. Gideon was directed to save the Israelites from Midian's hand. Samson was commanded to destroy the Philistines. Moses was chosen to lead the Israelites out of Egypt. Paul was appointed to proclaim the good news to the Gentiles. In each of these cases, God was the one who told them what He desired them to do.

Furthermore, it shared that God desires to have a relationship with us and also wants to personally reveal His individual plans with us.[2] This is in opposition to the more common practice of just thinking up on our own of how to please God. Jesus, Himself, did not even act without looking for His Father's direction. John 5:19 reinforces this idea as it says, "Jesus gave them this answer: 'Very truly I tell you, the Son can do nothing by himself; he can do only what he sees his Father doing, because whatever the Father does the Son also does.'" Jesus acts as a model for us since He always looked for His Father's cue before acting.[3]

Also Scripture supports this idea by referring to followers of Christ "children" or "slaves of God." Neither children nor slaves control what they are to do in their lives, but always look to their father or master for direction. In the same way, we are supposed to wait on the instructions of God.

When I realized these principles, they made a huge effect on my Christian walk. Instead of trying to witness to a person any time I felt like it, now I tried to share spiritual insights only whenever I perceived God working in a person's life or when I felt an inner prompting of the Spirit.

That didn't mean that I didn't continually witness to others. Instead, I attempted to stir up a desire for God in others by living in a Christ-like manner and by freely sharing with anyone how God was acting in my life. By doing these things, I shifted from focusing from telling others what they were missing by not knowing Christ to focusing on what was special about God in my own life. Then maybe they would become curious about God and start to ask me about the gospel and eventually yearn for a relationship with God. Additionally, I personally prayed for people and for opportunities to share my hope with them.

Also, instead of participating in activities that I believed would be pleasing to God, I tried to identify what God wanted to me to do for His kingdom. I carried this out in a variety of ways. I prayed and attempted to listen for His quiet voice. I read the Bible and tried to be sensitive to any verses that might jump out at me. I observed the circumstances around me and sought the counsel of other Christians.[4]

I specifically did this each summer when my children were young. I offered up a prayer, asking the Lord what activity He desired me to get involved with during the upcoming school year. Each year, I perceived some type of answer, such as volunteer at the local nursing home, be involved with "Mothers of Preschoolers," or join "Moms in Touch."

One particular spring, I prayed as usual, but did not feel as if I received an answer. This seemed rather odd to me since I usually felt as though I was always given some sort of direction. However, I quickly discovered why there had been silence. Three weeks later, my son John was diagnosed with cancer, so I ended up home schooling him the next school year. The Lord knew what was going to happen and that I would figure out shortly why He had been silent.

This event made me more confident in later years that the voice I usually heard was indeed from God. However, I still attempted to validate what I thought I was prompted to do. I looked to see if anything I felt called to do opposed Scripture. If it did, then I knew it wasn't from God. I looked for more than one confirmation to make sure I was following His will. Lastly, if I had a general peace about what I was being told to do, then I believed that it was from the Lord.[5] However, I still had to act on faith since I never had a guarantee. Yet, I figured if my heart's motivation was to please God, then He would surely intervene and block my actions if I was not on the right path.

I read in Hebrews 11:1, "Now faith is being sure of what we hope for and certain of what we do not see." This verse points to the idea that when we feel led to act upon something, we should do so even though there might not be much evidence to support it. One example of this principle is when Joshua was directed by God to tell the Israelites to cross the Jordan River during a time when it was at flood stage. The river's waters continued to rage as they were about to cross, and it appeared as if they would be swept away in the current. Yet, the priests put their feet into the water. Only when they acted on their beliefs and showed trust, did the water stop flowing.

I also thought back to Noah, who proceeded to build an ark even though no water seemed to be imminent. He had to stop everything he was doing at the time to follow God. Additionally, he had to put up with heckling from those around him who believed him to be foolhardy to undertake such a project. Thus, he truly had to believe that this project was what God wanted him to do. It was by faith Noah acted.

Therefore, I began to try to obey what God was directing me to do in my life, even though I had no proof that my deductions were correct. One such time was when a series of events really made me think that I was being directed to move to Austin, Texas and possibly marry a particular man.

The idea of moving to Austin first got planted in my mind when one of my friends moved there when her husband found a new job. When her family relocated to Austin, I was sort of envious. For years, I had had entertained the thought of moving to some place warmer and sunnier than Pittsburgh, and this new location sounded exciting.

Then about a year later, Austin again came to my attention. My daughter joined the Peace Corps and met a fellow volunteer the first day she arrived. His hometown was Austin, and he and my daughter developed a relationship while abroad. They eventually married a few years later once they had finished with the Peace Corps.

Also, during the time my daughter was getting to know this man from Austin, my son Peter informed me that he had obtained an internship with a company in Austin. While working there, he met Rachel, another intern at the same company. Rachel was from Austin and they began to date steadily. After Peter graduated from college, this company offered him a job, and he accepted the position and moved to Austin. He and Rachael got married two years later.

It was astonishing to me how this town, which was such a far distance from us, was continually impacting our family. I began to wonder if the Lord might be calling me to move to this particular area since it seemed my two oldest kids both met someone from there.

I decided to do some research about Austin, and I discovered that the University of Texas was located there. Surprisingly, and it had a family and consumer sciences department. Over the years, I had periodically looked for colleges that offered family and consumer sciences and contemplated moving to be near one. Although I didn't know if I would ever get a chance to teach at the college-level, I thought it still would be appealing to be close to a university that offered my discipline. *Was this another way God was directing me to move to Austin? Should I move during this upcoming summer?*

I discovered this information just before I was about to eat dinner with my two youngest boys, John and Paul. I called them to the table and we all sat down. As I began to eat, I silently mulled over how this would affect them. That would mean taking my youngest son of out of his senior year of high school. *Was it the right thing to do?*

Immediately after pondering these thoughts, I turned my head to the left and noticed a bottle of a seasoning called "Mrs. Dash" that was beside me on the table. Peter, my oldest son, had purchased it the last time he had been home. On top of it, in red letters, were the words, "Choose to Move." Although it was referring to an exercise regime, it stunned me how it seemingly was answering the question in my head.

I don't remember formally praying about moving, which thinking back, I guess I should have. Instead, I just had a general feeling not to move since Paul was at the top of his class and wanted to finish his senior year of playing volleyball with his team. Rightly or wrongly, I chose to stay in Pittsburgh and determined to put off thinking about moving again until after Paul graduated from high school.

After his graduation, I remembered how all my other children usually stayed connected to their high school classmates during their first summer home after college.

But then after that, each subsequent summer, they did not return home as they usually they went off and did internships or co-ops. I figured if I just stayed one more year, then I could move when it would be easier on Paul.

Over the next year or so, either the name Austin or Texas continually began to invade my surroundings. I was aware that you notice things more if you start looking for them, but it just seemed uncanny how often I saw the words '*Austin*' or '*Texas*.' I saw it mentioned in the newspaper, on plaques, the television, roadway signs, and on many other things. However, what surprised me the most was the number of cars that I saw with a Texas license plate, especially considering how far away this state was from Pennsylvania.

On one occasion, I began to scold myself for how silly I was that I always took seeing a Texas tag as being a sign that I was to move there. I had pulled up behind a car with a Maryland license plate. I thought, *"Here's a Maryland plate and I'm sure there are plenty of other states plates that I probably just don't notice."* Just as that thought came to me, a car drove pass me in the turning lane to my right that caught my attention. It had a Texas license plate. I laughed to myself. *Maybe I'm not nuts.*

Then, I met an interesting man online who was from Austin. It was the beginning of the previous Labor Day weekend, and I had a Christian radio station playing. An advertisement for a Christian matchmaking site aired, which offered free access for the upcoming holiday weekend. During the thirteen years that David had been gone, I would occasionally jump on various online dating websites just to see if there was anyone of interest. I usually didn't stay on long as I was only mildly curious.

This particular time, though, I set up a profile and perused some of the men without contacting anyone. The next day, I received an email from a pastor who was from the same part of Austin where my son Peter was living in Texas. I couldn't believe it. *What were the chances of someone responding to me who was from that particular area?* I wondered if God was signaling to me again to move to Austin.

This man had many of the qualities that I had on my "wish list." He was obviously quite spiritual, widowed, had a master's degree, and had five grown children, which made me think he enjoyed having family. He even liked to dance, which I also loved to do. All this piqued my interest. As we emailed back and forth, I was even more attracted because I discovered that he had a Baptist background with a Charismatic influence. I couldn't think of a more desirable spiritual outlook to match my own.

Since he had only been widowed for a few months, he cautioned me that he currently was only looking for friendship. To prevent getting close too quickly, he would only write every three days or so. Since he had everything I was looking for, and since over the years, so few men had ever come close to what I wanted, I found my heart quickly opening up to the possibility of a relationship between us. I could understand that he was in a far different place than me, but his slow responses were difficult, especially since I had been conditioned by the professor from the small Christian college to expect multiple email replies each day.

About a week or so later, after connecting with this gentleman and feeling neglected by the infrequent responses, I suddenly felt like I should end communications with him. Although I didn't understand why I had this strange feeling, I immediately emailed him that I no longer wanted to write to him. I reflected that since he was freshly widowed, he needed more time to investigate other possibilities anyway. I also believed if the Lord was truly orchestrating this, He could certainly reconnect us again at some later time.

A year after this, I was about to be living alone for the first time. My youngest son was about to head off for his first year of college, which meant all of my kids would be out of the house. Being widowed up to this point had been tolerable since I had always had my children around. However, being faced with living in an empty house frightened me. Since I was contemplating moving to Austin, I decided to try out living there. I went on Craigslist and found a woman who was looking to rent out one of the bedrooms in her house. She was about my same age and also about to experience the empty nest syndrome. After communicating with her a bit, I decided to stay from mid-October to mid-November, which was a time when I could be physically away from the main office of my cyber school.

A few weeks before going, I decided to go on a different Christian matchmaking site and post a profile, listing my current city as Austin in an effort to see if there were any interesting men available in this new area. As I browsed through the profiles from this region, I happened to notice the Austin pastor with whom I had communicated the previous year. I clicked on his profile, curious to see what he was now doing. After reading through it and then closing out of it, it immediately dawned on me that he would be able to see that I had reviewed it.

The next day, I received an email from him, asking me if I was the same woman who had written him a year ago. I confirmed I was and he asked me if I had moved to Austin. I explained to him about my plans to investigate if I really would like living in Texas. He told me to contact him when I was in town and maybe we could get together.

After I arrived in Austin I wrote him, but he made no effort to meet me. This frustrated me as Texas was quite a distance from where I lived and this would be the perfect opportunity to meet. I supposed that he was seeing someone else, but when I prayed about it, I believed rightly or wrongly to keep writing him every day during my stay, whether he wrote back or not. I did continue to write, but at the end of my matchmaking site membership, I quit and our interaction ended.

However, we connected again in another way. When I returned home, I decided to join Facebook because our church was using it to connect people together in doing certain activities. Since my church was encouraging everyone to read the Bible in one year, they had created a page on Facebook for people to discuss any reactions or experiences they had while pursuing this goal. Since I was interested in seeing what people would be writing, I set up a profile for myself. As I was signing up, a screen popped up suggesting various people that I might know so that I could 'friend' them, and his name was among those listed. I supposed that he had attempted to search for me on this social network earlier, so I added him as a friend, but we didn't converse very much.

Since months passed and I saw no interest from him to pursue a relationship with me, I prayed to the Lord that if we would not eventually be together, to free me of any thoughts of a life with him. The very next morning when I woke up, I turned on the TV. It was a Sunday morning and the channel I was set to showed Pastor Joel Olsteen giving a sermon. The first words out of his mouth were, "Are you single? Do you want to be married and it is not happening? Maybe you aren't ready."

Oh, please. It has only been fourteen years.

This pastor continued, "Maybe the other person isn't ready."

Since I had just made my prayer the night before and this was so closely dealing with what I had been praying about, I thought it could possibly be God answering me. Maybe we would eventually be together and He was telling me to be patient.

That spring, I decided to go to North Carolina for a month as John, my middle son, was living there. He had obtained an eight-month co-op position with a company in Raleigh. Besides, I always had thought North Carolina would be a nice warm location to live and I could see how I liked it the area. Additionally, my step-mother was in a nearby suburb, and I figured we could all be together for the Easter holiday and John's soon-approaching twenty-first birthday. I found a place to rent and ended up meeting new friends and thoroughly enjoying this beautiful region. However, in my heart, I still believed I that I was supposed to go to Austin and not Raleigh.

Shortly after returning home from this visit, I was outside my house doing some yard work. I noticed that my next door neighbor, Nikole, was also gardening so I struck up a conversation with her. She asked me how I had liked Raleigh, and I shared that I really liked that area of the country, but still felt that the Lord was still directing me to Austin. She then commented, "My sister and her husband had just put up their house up for sale three weeks ago and they want to move into this neighborhood. I know you have been thinking about moving. Would you be interested in selling your house to them? I don't know how long it is going to take to sell their house though."

I was totally shocked. I wondered if God was orchestrating a way to sell my house easily. I was having a difficult time just picking up and moving for my own desires but, if my move could help someone else out, then this would help me make this huge decision. It would be great if I didn't have to put my house up on the market and have troops of people coming through. Furthermore, I could save some money by not having to pay a realtor.

"That sounds like a great option! If possible though, I really would like to stay until the end of the summer. That way Paul could have this last summer at home," I replied.

"That would probably work. They haven't had anyone interested in their house yet and my mom has a big five-bedroom house where they could stay if their house sold earlier," she responded.

"Let them know that I'm definitely interested," I responded and I went home to get my house in order.

After a week or so, Nikole informed me that the previous night that her sister and her husband had just accepted an offer on their house. She wondered if they could look at my house that night. I agreed and they came over and browsed through my house. After viewing it they divulged that they were also considering another house. Their lack of enthusiasm made me think that they were not interested, and they did not end up buying my house. It had all seemed to be straight from the Lord, but for some reason, it didn't work out.

It was so difficult to tell if the Lord wanted me to move or not. Therefore, I decided to finish all the home improvement projects necessary and then put my house on the market to see what would happen. I would give the Lord from the end of August to Thanksgiving to bring me a buyer if that was His will. If it didn't sell, then I would remove my listing and just stay, believing that the Lord wanted me to remain where I was.

However, I had difficulty getting workers to my house to complete the projects that needed to be done. I called contractors who would either not get back to me or would set up an appointment and never show up. I had one painter cancel four times on me. Projects that got started seemed to take two to three times longer than anticipated. I never got my house on the market in time, as the big projects only got a few days before Thanksgiving. I felt like I was getting all these signs to move, but I was being blocked from selling my house.

It was frustrating not understanding what God wanted me to do, but I still felt like I was supposed to move to Texas at some point. I reflected back on what I took as a sign that I was supposed to move. That previous October, I had been walking in my neighborhood when I met up with a woman I casually knew named Katie. She was the president of "Women Aglow," a group of women filled with the Spirit who got together regularly to pray and do acts of charity. We got talking and she asked me if I was interested in going to any of their meetings and receiving their newsletter. I said I'd think about it, and I ended up giving her my email address.

A few weeks later, she sent out a group email asking if anyone had room to take in a woman in their group who was in need of a place to live. Since I was going to have an empty house with my last child going off to college, I felt I could offer one of my bedrooms to her. I emailed back to her telling her of that possibility. Katie emailed me back telling me that the woman already found a place. However, she said that she would pass on my name and telephone number in case things didn't work out.

I didn't think I would ever hear from this lady, whose name was Marge, but she ended up calling me several months later in January. I was in Florida with my boys, visiting my sister over Christmas break, when she called me on my cell phone. She told me that things weren't working out with her current living situation and maybe we could get together to talk about the possibility of her staying at my home. I shared that I was out of town and wouldn't be able to meet with her until after I got back home. She said fine and to call her when I arrived back home.

After getting off the phone with her, I started wondering why this woman was having such housing issues. I prayed and asked God if I should take this woman into my house. The answer I believed I received was "No." I decided to call this lady back. I didn't want to tie her up in finding a new place if I wasn't going to let her come live with me.

After relaying the answer I believed that I had received after praying, she pressed, "Are you sure you heard correctly?"

"All I can say is that when I have gone against what I believe the Lord is telling me, I have paid the price. I'm sorry," I replied.

"Ok. Can we get together sometime for lunch then?" she asked.

"Sure, that would be fine," I agreed.

Marge never called until the beginning of June and as promised, asked me to go out to lunch. I agreed and we met at a Chinese restaurant in the area. I was concerned that Marge was contacting me because she was interested in seeing if she could live with me. Since I had been contemplating moving to Austin but was hesitant to uproot my two youngest children, I thought about the possibility of maybe having her live in my house while I rented something in Austin. That way, I could just return home during my kid's college vacations.

When we met at the restaurant, I was determined to learn more about Marge and if she would be trustworthy enough to stay in my house alone. For about an hour, we talked and I was listening for clues the type of person she was. Because she was a member of the Women's Aglow organization, I figured she was a Christian that believed strongly in the workings of the Spirit, and I found that to be true. I also found out that she was divorced and had experienced some trials in her life, too. Then the conversation paused and totally diverged from what we had been discussing, Marge announced to me, "I feel like the Lord wants me to share a story with you. I have no idea why, but I will tell you."

I said, "Ok."

She asked, "Do you know who Marilyn Hinkey is?"

"I think I've heard of the name but I don't really know who she is," I responded.

"At one time in her life she felt the Lord offered her the choice to continue to be a teacher and stay where she was or to move, get married, and have a ministry." She paused and then emphasized, "I really don't know why I'm supposed to tell you this, but I just feel like the Lord is prompting me to share this with you."

Her short narrative sort of stunned me, so I confessed to her, "Well, I can see how it could apply to my life. Currently, I am a teacher and can remain where I am, but I've had a nudging to move to Austin for a while. There is also a guy who lives there that I met online that might be a God-ordained match for me. He is a widower who is spirit-filled pastor. However, I'm not really in contact with him right now."

"Oh, dear! Don't move there just because I told you this story. Whenever I'm trying to discern God's plan, I usually like to have three confirmations," Marge quickly cautioned.

"I'm not just reflecting upon what you have just stated, but there have been other indications as well," I assured her. I explained to her the other signs I thought I had received previously that seemingly were pointing me toward moving to Austin. I also revealed to her that there were some other things that made me think this guy in Austin was someone whom God had chosen for me.

"Then maybe that is what you are supposed to do. It is interesting that I just felt led by the Lord to go out to lunch with you. It is even more amazing that I even found your telephone number. It was just on a small scrap of paper," she informed me.

We talked a little longer, and when we finished our meals, we said goodbye and left. Upon arriving at home, I felt led to work on my book. I had been avoiding doing anything with it for the past few weeks but, now after having this spiritual conversation, I was more motivated to be obedient and spend some time working on it.

I decided to make a list of all the people who I had mentioned in my book and get their permission to use their names. I copied the sections where they were mentioned and emailed them to each and asked if I could include their real name or if they rather I made up a name for them. I was going back and forth from my manuscript to my email, when I noticed that I received a new email. It was from the pastor in Austin.

I had been writing him for the past two weeks. I believed the Lord had wanted me to share with him my thoughts about each of the classes on healing that I was taking at a local church. We had not been communicating much prior to this, but rightly or wrongly, I felt the Lord directed me to do this. I didn't expect him to answer, but proceeded, thinking that I was being obedient. Up to this point, I had written two messages without receiving a response.

I opened up his note and, after he apologized for the delay in getting back with me, he shared his thoughts about what I had written about the class. Then, at the bottom of the message, he divulged that the reason that our relationship had not progressed was because of the distance. However, he now recognized a potential for a relationship between us. The strange prophesy given to me by Marge and then receiving an email from this pastor in Texas on that very afternoon seem too coincidental. I took it as the Lord really was moving me toward a move and a possible relationship with this man.

We wrote back and forth over the next weeks, mostly discussing our thoughts about my reactions to each of the ideas presented in the remaining eight classes on healing. My ideas and those of this pastor began to deviate immensely and we finally ended up severing our connection. A few months later, I noticed on Facebook that he was engaged to another woman and later that he eventually married her.

This new development was not as upsetting to me as the fact that I had shared so many of these "coincidences" with others. I professed to others the possibility that the Lord was directing me to relocate to Austin and that this guy might be the one the Lord had planned for me. Since these indications that I was supposed to connect with this pastor came to nothing, I wondered if I was depending too much on looking for "signs." I feared that I was discrediting God to the people with whom I had shared my thoughts. *Would people doubt that one can be guided by God since my assumptions failed to pass?*

Yet, I reflected, wasn't faith moving in the direction that you believed the Lord was taking you, even when you didn't have any evidence? I had believed the Lord was directing me and trusted Him to correct me if that those leadings were incorrect.

The thought also came to me that maybe the Lord was just testing me. I reflected upon the instance in the Bible where God instructed Abraham to sacrifice his son, Isaac. As Abraham proceeded to carry out this plan, God stopped him. He was glad to see that Abraham placed nothing above Him, but didn't actually want him to carry out the plan. Maybe God was verifying if I would be willing to move from the town where I had lived most of my life and trust Him with my future. Maybe I was still to move, but the timing was not right. I didn't know. However, this event made me more humble in assuming what God's will is for my life, which is always a good thing.

Scripture

John 6:44: "No one can come to me unless the Father who sent me draws him, and I will raise him up at the last day."

Romans 6:22 (Italics added): But now that you have been set free from sin and have become *slaves to God*, the benefit you reap leads to holiness, and the result is eternal life.

John 1:12 (Italics added): Yet to all who received him, to those who believed in his name, he gave the right to become *children of God*.

1 Peter 2:16 (Italics added): Live as free men, but do not use your freedom as a cover-up for evil; live as *servants of God*.

1 John 3:1 (Italics added): How great is the love the Father has lavished on us, that we should be called *children of God*!

Amos 3:7: Surely the Sovereign LORD does nothing without revealing his plan to his servants the prophets.

Hebrews 11:1: Now faith is being sure of what we hope for and certain of what we do not see.

Joshua 3:14-16a: So when the people broke camp to cross the Jordan, the priests carrying the ark of the covenant went ahead of them. Now the Jordan is at flood stage

all during harvest. Yet as soon as the priests who carried the ark reached the Jordan and their feet touched the
water's edge, the water from upstream stopped flowing.

Genesis 22:2, 10-12: Then God said, "Take your son,
your only son, Isaac, whom you love, and go to the
region of Moriah. Sacrifice him there as a burnt offering
on one of the mountains I will tell you about."
    Then he reached out his hand and took the knife to
slay his son. But the angel of the LORD called out to him
from heaven, "Abraham! Abraham!"
    "Here I am," he replied.
    "Do not lay a hand on the boy," he said. "Do not do
anything to him. Now I know that you fear God, because
you have not withheld from me your son, your only son."

Lord Sharing with People Their Assignment

Genesis 6:13-14 (Giving assignment to Noah): So God
said to Noah, "I am going to put an end to all people, for
the earth is filled with violence because of them. I am
surely going to destroy both them and the earth. So make
yourself an ark of cypress wood; make rooms in it and
coat it with pitch inside and out."

Genesis 12:1-3 (Giving assignment to Abraham): The
LORD had said to Abram, "Leave your country, your
people and your father's household and go to the land I
will show you. " I will make you into a great nation and
I will bless you; I will make your name great, and you
will be a blessing. I will bless those who bless you, and
whoever curses you I will curse; and all peoples on earth
will be blessed through you."

Genesis 17:15-16 (Giving assignment to Abraham): God also said to Abraham, "As for Sarai your wife, you are no longer to call her Sarai; her name will be Sarah. I will bless her and will surely give you a son by her. I will bless her so that she will be the mother of nations; kings of peoples will come from her."

Genesis 37:5-9 (Giving assignment to Joseph):

Joseph had a dream, and when he told it to his brothers, they hated him all the more. He said to them, "Listen to this dream I had: We were binding sheaves of grain out in the field when suddenly my sheaf rose and stood upright, while your sheaves gathered around mine and bowed down to it." His brothers said to him, "Do you intend to reign over us? Will you actually rule us?" And they hated him all the more because of his dream and what he had said.

Then he had another dream, and he told it to his brothers. "Listen," he said, "I had another dream, and this time the sun and moon and eleven stars were bowing down to me."

Exodus 3:7-10 (Giving assignment to Moses):

The LORD said, "I have indeed seen the misery of my people in Egypt. I have heard them crying out because of their slave drivers, and I am concerned about their suffering. So I have come down to rescue them from the hand of the Egyptians and to bring them up out of that land into a good and spacious land, a land flowing with milk and honey—the home of the

Canaanites, Hittites, Amorites, Perizzites, Hivites and Jebusites. And now the cry of the Israelites has reached me, and I have seen the way the Egyptians are oppressing them. So now, go. I am sending you to Pharaoh to bring my people the Israelites out of Egypt."

Judges 6:14 (Giving assignment to Gideon): The LORD turned to him and said, "Go in the strength you have and save Israel out of Midian's hand. Am I not sending you?"

Judges 13:1-5 (Giving assignment to Samson):

Again the Israelites did evil in the eyes of the LORD, so the LORD delivered them into the hands of the Philistines for forty years. A certain man of Zorah, named Manoah, from the clan of the Danites, had a wife who was sterile and remained childless.The angel of the LORD appeared to her and said, "You are sterile and childless, but you are going to conceive and have a son. Now see to it that you drink no wine or other fermented drink and that you do not eat anything unclean, because you will conceive and give birth to a son. No razor may be used on his head, because the boy is to be a Nazirite, set apart to God from birth, and he will begin the deliverance of Israel from the hands of the Philistines."

1 Samuel 9:15-17 (Giving assignment to Saul): Now the day before Saul came, the LORD had revealed this to Samuel: "About this time tomorrow I will send you a man from the land of Benjamin. Anoint him leader over my people Israel; he will deliver my people from the hand of the Philistines. I have looked upon my people, for their cry has reached me."

When Samuel caught sight of Saul, the LORD said to him, "This is the man I spoke to you about; he will govern my people."

1 Samuel 16:1 (Giving assignment to David): The LORD said to Samuel, "How long will you mourn for Saul, since I have rejected him as king over Israel? Fill your horn with oil and be on your way; I am sending you to Jesse of Bethlehem. I have chosen one of his sons to be king."

1 Chronicles 28:5-6 (Giving assignment to Solomon): Of all my sons—and the LORD has given me many— he has chosen my son Solomon to sit on the throne of the kingdom of the LORD over Israel. He said to me: 'Solomon your son is the one who will build my house and my courts, for I have chosen him to be my son, and I will be his father.'

Jonah 1:1 (Giving assignment to Jonah): The word of the LORD came to Jonah son of Amittai: "Go to the great city of Nineveh and preach against it, because its wickedness has come up before me."

Luke 1:31-33 (Giving assignment to Mary): "You will be with child and give birth to a son, and you are to give him the name Jesus. He will be great and will be called the Son of the Most High. The Lord God will give him the throne of his father David, and he will reign over the house of Jacob forever; his kingdom will never end."

Acts 22:14-15 (Giving assignment to Paul): "Then he said: 'The God of our fathers has chosen you to know his will and to see the Righteous One and to hear words from his mouth. You will be his witness to all men of what you have seen and heard.

Obeying the Leading of the Holy Spirit

"The flight that you booked to Cincinnati on your way to Austin has been canceled, but we have put you on another. It has a connection through Cincinnati also and leaves five minutes later than your original booking," the airline official informed me when I arrived at the airline check-in desk.

"No big deal," I thought to myself. It was basically the same flight. I told her that was fine and she handed me a new ticket for Flight 1522. However, thirty minutes before this rescheduled flight was set to leave, an airline employee announced over the loudspeaker, "Flight 1522 scheduled for Cincinnati is experiencing mechanical issues. We are going to reschedule everyone onto other flights. Please come up to the desk as we call your name."

I was on my way to visit my son Peter and his wife, who had married six months earlier. I wondered if I would still be able to make my son's mother-in-law's birthday. She had invited me to join them for a dinner party when she heard that I was coming down to visit Peter. The flight problems didn't upset me too much, though. I had previously had heard horror stories from many of my friends about their flights being canceled, and this was only the first time I had encountered any issues with flying. Therefore, I just patiently waited for my turn. Twenty minutes passed before I was called to the desk.

"We have a flight that goes through your original connection of Cincinnati and will get you to Austin by nine tonight," the lady at the desk informed me.

"Well, I don't have to go through Cincinnati. Are there any flights going through different connecting cities that will get me to Austin any sooner?" I proposed.

"You could go through Chicago, and that will give you an arrival time of seven in Austin," the woman shared.

"That would be much better," I replied, and she booked me on this new flight. I was happy to have found a flight leaving at a reasonable time.

Whenever I flew, I had the habit of praying that God would seat me beside someone to whom I could witness. This time was no different, so as I waited to board, I silently prayed, "God, please put me beside whom you would choose."

As our flight was boarding, the woman checking the tickets warned me, "If you can't get your book bag into the overhead compartment, you will have to check it. Just bring it back here and I'll give you a tag for it. You can reclaim it just as soon as you get off the flight." I hoped that would not happen, since I had my laptop stored in my book bag.

As I boarded, I immediately understood why I had been given such an admonition, as the aircraft was one of the smallest I had ever seen. The plane was only wide enough for two seats on one side of the aisle and only one on the other. I quickly found my seat and discovered that I was beside the window and in the adjoining seat sat an older woman.

I glanced at the overhead storage area. Indeed, it looked inadequate for my carry-on, but I tried to hoist it into the cramped space anyway. Despite my best efforts to make the bag fit, I could see that it was not going to happen and plopped it down into the aisle.

"Why didn't you just ship that?" my seatmate snapped. Her remark really annoyed me. *How did I know I was going to be on this small plane?* Besides, I most certainly would not have sent my computer ahead to my final destination. I said nothing, but quietly extracted my computer and put it on my seat and went to the front of the plane to check my bag. When I returned, I sat down, most unhappy to be seated beside such an irritable woman and waited for the remaining passengers to board.

When the woman assigned to the seat across the aisle arrived toting a large computer case, she also attempted to wedge her bag into the overhead storage without success. Again my seatmate again barked, "You should have just shipped that!" She didn't really acknowledge the comment but looked over and saw that my seat had a little extra room in front.

She asked me, "Could I exchange seats with you? I believe my computer case will fit under in the space in front of you."

I quickly agreed and thought to myself, *"No problem!"* I was ecstatic to get away from this grumpy passenger. As the other woman switched seats with me and then struggled to squeeze the case underneath the seat, the unhappy lady remarked with exasperation, "I don't have any room for my feet. I suppose I'll just have to suffer."

"Is she going to complain about everything for the rest of the flight?" I wondered.

I was thrilled with my new seat, as it positioned me farther away from this cranky woman who thankfully was now reading a book. Because of this ordeal, I had forgotten that I had prayed to sit beside someone to whom I could witness. Instead, I began to read a book of my own entitled *Greater Works*.[1] It was a compilation of sermons by an eighteenth-century preacher named Smith Wigglesworth. Its main focus was on the miraculous gifts the Holy Spirit had bequeathed to the author and how others could acquire them also.

Later, as our flight neared its destination, I felt the Holy Spirit prompting me to ask the disagreeable woman if I could buy her dinner. *"No!"* I silently rebelled in my mind. *Did God truly want me to deal with that woman?* I had been quite eager to get away from her!

I hesitated, sure the woman would think I was nuts. After all, I was just a complete stranger. Then, I reflected upon the other times in my life when I had disobeyed what I thought the Lord was directing me to do. I always felt so miserable and unhappy afterward. *"Oh, all right!"* I silently pouted. Maybe this was the end of her trip and she did not have a connection and would want to head home instead. Maybe she would just say no.

As I was mustering up the courage to ask her, one of the flight attendants began to list the connecting gates over the loudspeaker. The irritable woman looked at her tickets. *"She does have a connection,"* I noticed. I needed to act now if I was going to ask at all. I leaned over the aisle.

"Excuse me—I was wondering if I could buy you dinner?" I asked the woman. My comment seemed to fluster her.

"Oh, no!" she replied hastily.

Then almost automatically, I placed my hand on her arm and say, "I believe you are hurting, and the Lord wants me to tell you that He sees you and wants you to know that He loves you." This action even shocked me, and I supposed that the Holy Spirit prompted me to do this because it just sort of happened without any forethought on my part.

She quickly turned her head and looked forward and would not look at me again. I was relieved. I had fulfilled what I believed the Lord had instructed me to do and just waited quietly as the plane made its way to the terminal. When we were parked at the gate, people began to rise and gather their things and make their way off the plane. When it came time for the woman to leave, she arose, turned to me, and said, "Thank you," and then deplaned.

While I did not know the woman's situation or circumstances, the sincerity I heard in the woman's now timid voice suggested to me that the Lord had surely given me those words to say. I was thankful I had taken the risk to follow the Lord's leading and didn't let my intimidation hinder me. I felt joy thinking that the Lord had entrusted me to help encourage her and to let her know that He cared for her. I prayed that she would now draw close to Him to find strength for whatever issues were facing her.

Scripture

Isaiah 30:21: Whether you turn to the right or to the left, your ears will hear a voice behind you, saying, "This is the way; walk in it."

John 15:10: "If you obey my commands, you will remain in my love, just as I have obeyed my Father's commands and remain in his love."

—30—

God's Purposes for Our Lives

G od has purposes for each person's life. Rick Warren emphasized this concept when he authored the book, *The Purpose Driven Life*. In this work, Warren exposes that our destiny is not just to be born, make a living, have some relationships, and then die. We have been created for much deeper aims.

Warren defines that mankind has five different purposes. The first purpose is to dedicate everything that you do to God, while being continually connected to Him as you do this. Secondly, God wants you to grow in love for others by being involved in close relationships and to do this on a regular basis. The third purpose is to shape our character so that we are more Christ-like. The fourth purpose is to use our God-given gifts to serve other believers in our church family. The fifth and last purpose is to introduce unbelievers to God.[1]

However, God has given people the freedom of choice to accomplish these purposes or not. Scripture shows Jonah sought to run away from his God-given task of preaching to the straying people of Nineveh. Samson failed to fully complete his commission of ridding Israel of the Philistine influence because his pride and self-indulgence. King Saul attempted to please God by acting upon what he thought would be acceptable to God rather than being obedient to what God had ordered.

Almost thirteen years ago, I began to perceive what I believed was part of the Lord's purpose for my life. I felt that He wanted me to share with others some of the ways He had worked in my life. Specifically, I believed He was directing me to write a book. I did not enjoy writing though and was reluctant to start.

Years began to pass, but every time I prayed about what I should be doing for the kingdom, the answer was always the same— *"Write the book."* I attempted to ignore this gentle prodding until it gradually became a burden to me, and I feared that I was being disobedient.

I had read somewhere that often the assignment God gives people is usually beyond what they are capable of accomplishing on their own. That way, after the task is completed, it will be God who receives the glory and not them. The exchange between Moses and God in Exodus 4:10-13 exemplifies this idea. After God instructed Moses to lead the Israelites out of Egypt, Moses repelled this directive stating, "'Pardon your servant, Lord. I have never been eloquent, neither in the past nor since you have spoken to your servant. I am slow of speech and tongue.' The LORD said to him, 'Who gave human beings their mouths? Who makes them deaf or mute? Who gives them sight or makes them blind? Is it not I, the LORD? Now go; I will help you speak and will teach you what to say.' But Moses said, 'Pardon your servant, Lord. Please send someone else.'"

After this exchange, God was full of anger. In His graciousness though, He appointed Aaron, Moses' brother, to be his spokesperson. However, negative repercussions followed as Aaron eventually ended up rebelling against Moses.

I reflected upon Moses' plight as I considered hiring someone else to do the writing for me. I decided I better attempt to write it on my own and depend on God to help. Anyway, maybe this project wasn't going to be for mass consumption. Possibly, it was just to help develop myself in some fashion. However, if others eventually did read it and find it useful, then the glory would certainly be the Lord's.

I finally began writing while visiting my sister's over Easter. I just picked up a notebook and a pencil and started to write. I thought if I could just get something down, I could fine tune it later.

Producing a book solely about my life stories seemed so self-centered, even if my intention was to reveal God's glory. Therefore, I initially included a separate spiritual lesson to accompany each section. Then, I followed each chapter with associated verses to validate the ideas presented.

As I worked on this project, I made endless revisions, which made me feel so incompetent to accomplish this feat. Then, God seemingly sent someone to encourage me. Sandy, a newly elected deaconess at our church said, "I have been assigned to pray for some members of the congregation and I chose you to be one of those people. What prayer concerns do you have?" I shared with her my struggles over writing this book and she responded, "I've heard that writing a book is like developing your muscles. You just have to keep revising a manuscript to get it right just like you have to continually flex your muscles to strengthen them." Her advice gave me hope that no one was able to just put something down on paper and have it perfect the first time.

I continued to work on the stories and lessons for about six years. Then, through an odd set of circumstances, a man from a large Christian organization asked to read what I had composed so far. After going through it, he commented that it was rather lengthy and maybe that I should remove the lessons and just make them into some sort of devotional. It seemed like God was directing me back to my original calling—to write my story. However, I decided to include some brief spiritual insights into each of the narratives.

God also revealed to me that I was to use a pen name to publish the book. The idea arose on my airplane flight home from my sister's after first starting to write. I noticed a man sitting in the row ahead of me across the aisle that was reading Scripture. Since I rarely ever witnessed anyone reading a Bible in public and admired anyone who was passionate enough about their faith to do so, I pondered if I should say anything to this fellow believer. Finally, as I saw him close the book, so I called over to him, "Excuse me, are you a Christian?" We ended up conversing for a while about our faith, and eventually, I timidly confided in him that I was attempting to author a book about my spiritual experiences.

"Are you going to use your real name?" he asked. The thought to write under a name other than my own never crossed my mind. Using a pseudonym seemed so untruthful to me, but it got me thinking that maybe the Lord was giving me a sign to write under a name other than my own.

Years later, the Lord seemed to go further and reveal what this actual name should be. When I took my van to the car dealership for a scheduled maintenance, the service manager behind the desk thought he recognized me.

"Hey, did you go to high school around here? You look so familiar," he questioned.

"I graduated from North Rivers High School," I responded, revealing that I had attended one of the local school districts.

"What was your maiden name?" he continued.

"Wolff." I answered.

"What is your middle name?" he asked.

I replied, "Chadwick," thinking it was strange that he would think that would help him remember who I was.

"Mary Chadwick Wolff—that sounds like a writer!" he exclaimed. Now, I know what it means when a mouth drops open in astonishment, because that is exactly what mine did. Totally stunned, I wondered what had prompted this service manager to suggest that my full maiden name, of all names, had the ring of an author to it. Rightly or wrongly, I believed this was this God's confirmation that I should indeed write under a pen name, as the man on the plane had suggested.

After writing for eight years, I was very weary of this project. All told, I had well over 400 pages. Never really enjoying this venture to begin with, I just wanted to be done. I knew it needed more work, but I found a Christian editor and sent off my stories to her to fine-tune. When I got it back a few months later, I saw that I needed to make a few modifications. I felt intimidated touching the manuscript now that no one would be checking my corrections. *What if I make mistakes when I make the changes?*

I enlisted the help of my youngest son, Paul, to look over my corrections. After beginning, he asked me if I was interested in more extensive revisions. I gladly agreed, but hoped that he would not take too long so that I could use the rest of the summer to finish.

Since I thought I was nearing the completion of this book, I looked into self-publishing it. I inquired for more information from one company that looked promising. Since they had my email address, they used it to send me notifications about discounts on their various options for publishing. One particular offer sounded good, so I signed up for it. Reading through the contract, I noticed that it required the manuscript to be submitted within one year. I thought nothing of that since I believed that I was almost done. However, that soon became an issue.

Paul was doing such a detailed job and because he was also another summer job, it took much more time than I thought it would. He didn't end up completing it until the last day of his summer break. Since my cyber school teaching job was about to begin again, I feared that I would have a difficult time revising my book and teaching at the same time. I contemplated taking time off of my job to really put the effort forth to make it more readable. Then, some events occurred that to support the idea that I should resign from my job to finish on the book.

Year to year, I never was guaranteed my teaching position, although, up to this point, it always was offered to me. I usually received a letter in the mail about a month before the start of school verifying my employment. This year, though, the teachers had unionized over the summer, and I didn't get my teaching schedule until two weeks prior to the start of school. As I read over it, I discovered that I was going to be teaching more classes, but that my pay was going to be reduced. This, understandably, was not pleasing to me. *Was the Lord helping me to take the leap of faith to resign and just solely concentrate on my writing now?* I knew I could not do a proficient job of revising my book if I was still teaching, so I resigned from my position at the end of the first semester. After having a break from writing and having time to focus solely upon the book, I approached my writing task with much more passion and almost enjoyed working on it.

After making significant changes, I was not excited to pay someone again to have my book edited. However, I felt the Lord provide an alternative option for me. Over the past year, I had become involved in ballroom dancing, and was at a dance when I noticed a guy who danced well. I hoped that he would ask me to dance and astonishingly, several songs later, he came over. Much to my surprise, the second question he asked was, "Are you a writer?"

I was stunned. I returned, "You haven't asked me my name or where I live. You don't know me at all. Why in the world would you ask me that?"

"I don't know. You just look artsy," he explained. After I told him that, in fact, I was currently writing a book, he told me how much he enjoyed writing. Then he asked, "What is your book about?" After describing my project, I found out that he also was a fellow Spirit-filled Christian.

Over the next few months, Bob and I got to know each other better. One night, as we were talking on the phone, he confessed that now that he was retired, he was seeking a purpose in his life. The next day, it dawned upon me that possibly he had entered my life to be the person who could review my book. I thought back to his joy in writing and discovered that he had been the valedictorian of his high school class. It seemed that he was rather well suited for such a task. The next time we talked, I asked him if he would look at the book and he said he would. Therefore, I began to email him a chapter a day to review. Tirelessly, he read all the chapters, and once a week, he gave me his input when we would meet. Bob was able to go through the entire book and I was thankful for his hard work.

I had Paul review it again, who made more revisions. When I looked over it again, I couldn't refrain from making even more changes. As my deadline was fast approaching, I prayed that the Lord would have a hand on the final version.

I reflected back over the years of trying to complete this project. It amazed me how the Lord seemingly had guided me through undertaking this project. He had pointed me back to focus on my personal story, revealed the pen name I should use, and provided people to edit it. I felt blessed to be part of His project and prayed that His purpose would be fulfilled through it.

It is my personal hope that you perceive how much God desires to be part of your life and is continually knocking at the door of your heart. If you open it up to Him, He will reach down from heaven and work powerfully in your life. He promises to be there every step of the way and support you, especially as you draw close to Him by praying and reading His Word. Then may you find the power of *living Scripture* in your own life!

Scripture

Psalm 139:13-16: For you created my inmost being; you knit me together in my mother's womb. I praise you because I am fearfully and wonderfully made; your works are wonderful, I know that full well. My frame was not hidden from you when I was made in the secret place, when I was woven together in the depths of the earth. Your eyes saw my unformed body; all the days ordained for me were written in your book before one of them came to be.

Exodus 9:16: But I have raised you up for this very purpose, that I might show you my power and that my name might be proclaimed in all the earth.

Philippians 2:13: For it is God who works in you to will and to act according to his good purpose.

1 Timothy 2:7: And for this purpose I was appointed a herald and an apostle—I am telling the truth, I am not lying—and a true and faithful teacher of the Gentiles.

Epilogue

I s your life full of experiences that seem orchestrated by God that make you amazed or do your days pass by, each the same as the last? Maybe you are overwhelmed by some trial in your life, and do not know how you are going to make it through another day. Take comfort, for God has a plan for your life that He fashioned even before you were born.

However, He has given you the freedom to follow this intended design for your life or to carry it out your own way. To allow God to direct you, you first must have a personal relationship with him. However, mankind was born with a sinful nature that goes against what God desires for us. When we act in ways contrary to what God wants, it blocks our connection with Him. We then need to restore our bond with our Lord for Him to guide us.

In Old Testament times, our relationship with Him was re-established through shedding the blood of an animal that was without blemish. In the fullness of time, God allowed Jesus, His perfect Son, to descend to earth and die on the cross as the final sacrifice for mankind's sins. Therefore, in this present time, anyone who acknowledges that they are incapable of living life as God intended it to be, and vows to submit the direction of their life to our Lord, will gain everlasting life with God.

Once you have arrived at this place, the Bible continually calls us to love and obey God. When you love someone, you spend time with them. So, dedicating part of your day to God is necessary for a full relationship with Him, and you cannot obey unless you know what God's desires are. To accomplish these directives, you need to be reading His Word and praying to Him on a consistent basis.

I found that when I just randomly picked up the Bible and started reading, I had the tendency to read the same passages over and over again, not learning anything. Then, I came across a method that helped me avoid this pitfall. I got a college-ruled, spiral notebook and started with the book of Matthew. As I read, I wrote down each verse until I filled an entire page. The next day, I continued from where I left off and filled another page. I continued to do this Monday through Saturday until I went through the entire Bible. When I finished one version of the Bible, I moved onto another version. Along with freeing me up from having to come up with what I would read each day, it also firmly established Scripture into my mind.

In regards to praying, this practice is merely talking to God. You should pray throughout your day as you draw closer to the Lord. It should consist of praising, thanking, confessing misbehaviors, and petitions. Then, time should be spent on listening for God to communicate with you. This will prove more fruitful if you can get away from distractions so that you are able to perceive God's quiet, still voice.

At first, the answers that you believe you receive from God might seem like you are talking to yourself. However, like anything else, the more you engage in an activity, the better you become at discerning His voice. A good test of whether the voice you hear is from God or an evil source is to ask, "Did Jesus die for our sins?" One Corinthians 12:3 verifies this method as it states, "Therefore I tell you that no one who is speaking by the Spirit of God says, 'Jesus be cursed,' and no one can say, 'Jesus is Lord,' except by the Holy Spirit."

When you enter into prayer, Satan will attempt to distract you and make your mind wander. Just realize that this is normal. Then try to refocus and start again.

Maybe you have declared yourself to be a Christian and participate in these activities but still seem to be living a mundane spiritual life. Have you ever been baptized with the Spirit? Culturally, this practice seems to be infrequently practiced in mainstream Christianity. Yet this practice is outlined in the New Testament without any mention of its inapplicability for today. It is a method for supercharging the Spirit in your life.

To receive this blessing, you can either turn to a Catholic church that offers a Life in the Spirit seminar or find a Spirit-filled church where this practice is embraced. I promote a group approach, since Scripture seems to indicate this blessing is usually bestowed by having someone put their hands upon another. However, ultimately, if you pray to the Lord, He will fashion events to lead you in receiving this sanctification.

Another thing to consider if you are not experiencing a full life is to ask yourself if you are being courageous.

Have you heard the Lord directing you to do something, but then were too fearful to step out and accomplish it? The Lord asks us to trust Him. However, what He asks usually seems risky, as He longs for you to depend upon Him and not your own abilities. He wants to test you to see if you trust Him. He wishes to glorify Himself by accomplishing things that you cannot do by yourself. You may even have to face ridicule from others as they question your "irrational" actions. It takes courage to do what the Lord is directing you to do. Therefore, the tendency is to remain on the safe and already known path. Yet, when we do that, we can fall short of what God wants for us and rob Him of the glory He deserves.

God desires you to have an exciting life, one where you see the Lord perform incredible feats that go far beyond what you can do on your own. If you have the determination and fortitude to draw close and follow Him, God will direct your life so that it is the most satisfying. He will also support you through trials that will develop your character. You will even come to view these challenges as a blessing, as they transform you closer into God's image. Begin today so that you will lead a fulfilling life, one where you accomplish something of eternal value and bring glory to God.

Endnotes

Chapter 3: Angels

1. Billy Graham, *Angels: God's Secret Agents* (Edison: Inspirational Press, 1986), 24.

Chapter 5: Speaking in Tongues

1. Robert Heidler, *Experiencing the Spirit* (Ventura: Regal Books, 1998), 136.

Chapter 6: Understanding the Bible

1. Josh McDowell, *The New Evidence that Demands a Verdict* (Nashville: Thomas Nelson Publishers, 1999), 4-6.
2. George Konig, "Science vs. the Bible," *100prophecies.org*, http://www.therefinersfire.org/science_bible.htm (accessed 4 April 2011).
3. David Wise, "The First Book of Public Hygiene," *Answersingenesis.org*, http://www.answersingenesis.org/creation/v26/i1/hygiene.asp (accessed 4 April 2011).

Chapter 8: Submission

1. Nee Watchman, *Authority and Submission* (Anaheim: Living Stream Ministry, 1988), 15.
2. Watchman 17.
3. Watchman 25-26.
4. Watchman 28-30.
5. Watchman 125, 132.
6. Watchman 172.
7. Watchman 39-40.
8. Watchman 100.

Chapter 21: Crying Out to the Lord in Prayer

1. Bill Gothard, *The Power of Crying Out* (Sisters: Multnomah Publishers, 2002), 12, 72.

Chapter 23: Power in Jesus' Name

1. Jessica Meyers, "Frisco store owner uses name of Jesus to stop robber," *DallasNews.com*, http://www.dallasnews.com/news/community-news/frisco/headlines/20100113-Frisco-store-owner-uses-name-of-5631.ece (accessed 30 June 2011).
2. "Would-be robber in Frisco flees in the name of Jesus," *DallasNews.com*, http://www.dallasnews.com/video/?bcid=221076404001 (accessed 30 June 2011).
3. David Regan, "Praying in the Name of Jesus," *Learn the Bible*, http://www.learnthebible.org/praying-in-the-name-of-jesus.html (Accessed 19 April 2011).
4. Gordon H. Richards, "Name of Jesus," *Love Without Borders Ministries, Inc.*, http://www.jesus4you.com/NameOfJesus1.htm (accessed 14 April 2011).

5. Gordon H. Richards, "Name of Jesus," *Love Without Borders Ministries, Inc.*, http://www.jesus4you.com/ NameOfJesus1.htm (accessed 14 April 2011).

6. Philip Yancy, *Prayer: Does It Make a Difference?* (Grand Rapids: Zondervan, 2006), 223-224.

7. Philip Yancy, *Prayer: Does It Make a Difference?* (Grand Rapids: Zondervan, 2006), 226-228.

8. Gordon H. Richards, "Name of Jesus," *Love Without Borders Ministries, Inc.*, http://www.jesus4you.com/ NameOfJesus1.htm (accessed 14 April 2011).

Chapter 24: God's Permissive Will

1. June Hunt, "Decision Making: Discerning the Will of God," *Hope for the Heart Biblical Counseling Keys*, 2002, 3.

Chapter 27: Healing

1. Smith Wigglesworth, *Greater Works* (New Kensington: Whitaker House, 2000), 11.

2. Darren Wilson, *Finger of God*, Wonderlust Productions, 2007.

3. Craig Groeschel, "God Wants You Happy," *Life-Church.tv*, http://www.lifechurch.tv/watch/urban-legends/2, (accessed 12 March 2011).

4. Dr. Chauncey Crandall and Pat Robertson, "Raising the Dead", *CBN.com*, http://www.cbn.com/media/player/index.aspx?s=/vod/DrChaunceyCrandall_091510_WS (accessed 11 April 2011).

5. Watchman Nee. *Spiritual Authority* (New York: Christian Fellowship Publishers, Inc., 1972), 16.

Chapter 28: Acting on Faith

1. Henry T. Blackaby and Claude V. King, *Experiencing God* (Nashville: LifeWay Press, 1999), 32.
2. Henry Blackaby and Richard Blackaby, *Experiencing God* (Nashville: LifeWay Press, 1999), 43.
3. Henry Blackaby and Richard Blackaby, *Experiencing God* (Nashville: LifeWay Press, 1999), 13-16.
4. Henry Blackaby and Richard Blackaby, *When God Speaks* (Nashville: LifeWay Press, 1995), 24, 39, 66, 79.

Chapter 29: Obeying the Leading of the Holy Spirit

1. Smith Wigglesworth, *Greater Works* (New Kensington: Whitaker House, 2000).

Chapter 30: God's Purposes for Our Lives

1. Rich Warren, *The Purpose Driven Life* (Grand Rapids: Zondervan, 2002), 67, 124, 173, 229-230, 281-282.